CW01079753

THE
YOUNG CRICKETERS'
YEARBOOK

THE
YOUNG CRICKETERS' YEARBOOK

BY GORDON ROSS

Queen Anne Press

A *Queen Anne Press* BOOK

© Queen Anne Press 1984

First published in Great Britain
in 1984 by Queen Anne Press,
Macdonald & Co (Publishers) Ltd,
Maxwell House, 74 Worship Street,
London EC2A 2EN

A BPCC plc company

The Young cricketer's yearbook.
  1. Cricket—Juvenile literature
  2. Cricket—Periodicals
  796.35'8'05   GV911

  ISBN 0–256–10526–1

Cover photograph by Russell Bass
taken at the Bank of England
ground at Roehampton.

Design by Rita Wuethrich.

Typeset by J & L Composition Ltd,
Filey, North Yorkshire

Reproduced, printed and bound in
Great Britain by
Hazell, Watson & Viney Limited,
Member of the BPCC Group,
Aylesbury, Bucks

CONTENTS

CREDITS

The cartoons on pages 67 and 70 are by the late Royman Browne, for many years the artist for *Playfair Cricket Monthly*, whose brilliant career was cut short by his untimely death.

The photographs on pages 11, 15, 22, 25, 35, 37, 39, 41, 57, 59, 63, 65, 78, 80, 88, 145, 147 are reproduced courtesy of Bill Smith; those on pages 55, 56, 77, 107, 109 and 126 courtesy of Central Press Photos Ltd.; those on pages 73, 74, 101, 102 and 137 courtesy of Marylebone Cricket Club; those on pages 75, 82, 87, 105, 113, 117, 125, 128, 141 and 142 courtesy of S & G Press Agency Ltd.; that on page 85 courtesy of Patrick Eagar; those on pages 91, 93 and 94 courtesy of Jim Parks; that on page 111 courtesy of Universal Pictorial Press; those on pages 115, 122 and 123 courtesy of Reuters; that on page 118 courtesy of the *Daily Mail* Manchester; that on page 30 courtesy of Brian and Elizabeth Nicholls; that on page 120 courtesy of *The Cricketer Quarterly*; that on page 131 courtesy of Bill Frindall; that on page 149 courtesy of *The Illustrated Sporting and Dramatic News*; that on page 35 courtesy of Scarborough and District Newspapers Ltd; those on pages 18, 20 and 43 courtesy of Harrison Worth Photography.

INTRODUCTION

The Young Cricketers' Yearbook is something new among a welter of cricket publications which crowd the bookshops these days. It is designed as a book of entertainment for the young cricket enthusiast, boy or girl, player or television viewer. Some of this summer's schools cricket competitions are featured and most exciting of all is the choice of Five Young Cricketers of The Year, just as *Wisden Cricketers' Almanack* always includes Five Cricketers of The Year from the first-class game. The final choice of these young players has been extremely difficult, and could not have been accomplished without the tremendous co-operation of the English Schools Cricket Association and its hardworking Secretary, Cyril Cooper. We wish these five boys every possible success. They may be seen in first-class cricket and, who knows, some of them may play for England.

They, and all aspiring cricket captains, will do well to read Trevor Bailey's fine article on captaincy. Trevor is one of the best tacticians in the game of cricket. Keith Andrew, Director of coaching, tells you of opportunities that exist for young players in the game; David Evans, a current Test match umpire, explains some of his problems, and Jim Parks, the former England wicket-keeper, talks about touring abroad. The master statistician, Bill Frindall, takes you behind the scenes into his magic world of figures. You will have heard Bill often in the Test Match Special BBC commentary team giving the answers to just about every possible question on cricket.

There is much more, too, within these pages. The Story of Cricket, The Story of One-Day Cricket, Strange Happenings on the Cricket Field, Curiosities at Lord's by Stephen Green, the Curator of the famous Lord's museum, Great Players, Great Matches, The Funny Men of Cricket, The Brave Men, a comprehensive statistical section and a Quiz with some very good prizes.

The book is not intended as a coaching book, but there is still plenty to learn in these pages about the game and playing it. There is fun, too, in what we might call – 'A Young Cricketer's Bedside book'. So begin reading the book now and see for yourself, and don't forget to send an entry for the Quiz.

Gordon Ross

Here is our Prize-winning

Quiz

1 What is the maximum number of runs that can be scored off a six-ball over?
2 Name an England, Australian and West Indies wicket-keeper.
3 What is the highest individual score made by an England player in a Test Match?
4 Which county won the Gillette Cup most times?
5 Which was the first county to win the NatWest Bank Trophy?
6 Can a fielder stand as close as he likes to a batsman?
7 Which of the two umpires is likely to no-ball a bowler for throwing?
8 Which England bowler took 19 wickets in a single Test Match?
9 Which English county has a fox as its crest?
10 Who were known as **The Three W's** when they played for the West Indies?
11 Which was the last country to come into Test cricket?
12 Name two England cricket captains who were not born in England.
13 How many first-class cricket counties are there?
14 Name five England Test Match grounds.
15 Which county match is known as **The Roses Match?**
16 Name two Minor counties which begin with 'C'.
17 Name three English seaside places where first-class cricket is played.
18 Which two schools play each other every year at Lord's?
19 How many overs are allowed per innings in a John Player League match?
20 Which country at present holds the Prudential World Cup?

Address your entries to
The Young Cricketers Yearbook
Quiz
Queen Anne Press
Macdonald & Co (Publishers) Ltd
Maxwell House
74 Worship Street
London EC2A 2EN

Closing date 31 December 1984. Entries will not be examined before this date.

The first twelve correct entries opened will receive a prize
That decision is final and binding and no correspondence will be entered into. Employees of Macdonald & Co (Publishers) Ltd and their families will not be eligible to compete. Only one entry per person will be accepted.

The prizes will include two cricket bats (one presented by Gray Nicolls, and one by National Westminster Bank); A gold Papermate pen and pencil set (presented by Gillette); a year's subscription to *The* Cricketer (presented by *The Cricketer* magazine); a selection of Queen Anne Press cricket books; a day out for two at any cricket match of your choice in 1985 as guests of Queen Anne Press.

What is ESCA?

BY CYRIL COOPER, GENERAL SECRETARY

He tells you exactly what it is

In my study I have a water-colour painting of a derelict blacksmith's shop in Dorset, a memory of the trade and home of my ancestors. As a young boy I spent much time in this forge at the end of the summer holidays after watching Philip Mead batting for days on end for Hampshire. In 1948 an historic meeting took place at 'The Jolly Blacksmith' in Twickenham, and ESCA was born.

What could be more natural, then, than the fact that I am now General Secretary of ESCA (or indeed that ESCA was the name of a successful racehorse in the sixties)?

But you still have not been told what ESCA is. Since you are reading this article, you are probably a member of ESCA yourself. Your school will be part of its County Schools' Cricket Association, which in turn will be part of ESCA. Too many capital letters? Yes, but it is easier to say 'ESCA' than 'English Schools' Cricket Association'. So ESCA is Schools' Cricket.

I have been involved in the organisation of the game for many years, and remember with fondness those halcyon days just after the last war when all the schools in my area of North Hampshire played cricket almost all the time – double summer time, too! Since then I have seen Mike Gatting score 116 in forty six minutes, Ian Botham take 7 for 37, John Lever help to dismiss Hampshire for 28 by 12.30 on a sultry, thundery morning in Essex, and a small boy from Reading appear from nowhere, bat number 7 for Berkshire and score 126 – Gordon Greenidge by name. At the time they were all under fifteen. The list is endless.

But now to 1984. Forty six county associations form the backbone of ESCA, running their own competitions, coaching courses and representative matches. A record number of county matches was played this summer. London Schools had over 100 matches, Cornwall over seventy, while every other county had matches at all levels from Under 19 to Under 11.

The Lord's Taverners

No article on schoolboy cricket can be written without mentioning the wonderful support the Lord's Taverners give to Youth Cricket, under the guidance of Director Tony Swainson. They support ESCA financially; their Under 19 Selective Coaching Course bridges the gap between schools' cricket and the first-class game; The Cricketer Colts Trophy had the magnificent total of over 1,600 schools taking part, with a final at Edgbaston.

Gordon Greenidge, just one of the great successes whom Cyril Cooper remembers when Gordon was Under 15. There are many more.

Under 19 Cricket

The aim of every boy must be to play for the English Schools' team in internationals, or go on tour perhaps to India or Zimbabwe, or play at Lord's in the Schools Cricket Week. Michael Gerard, a young London business man, has sponsored the Home Internationals for two years.

Barclays Bank Cup

Cricket in the comprehensive schools has been given a boost by the sponsorship of Barclays Bank for an Under 17 Cup. All types of schools are eligible for this trophy, and this year just under 500 teams took part, with the four semi-finalists being invited to London for the closing stages on the Bank's ground.

The United Friendly Festival

From the large number of Under 15 county games, four regional sides are chosen for a week's Festival Cricket. This competition has now been going for some years and many a county 'cap' had his first taste of representative cricket at this level. ESCA is fortunate that the United Friendly Insurance plc are sponsors of this week for the third year.

Esso Festivals

We are well aware how necessary it is for young boys to be introduced to the game so that they are able to share in its enthusiasms. We have found that the introduction of the 8-a-side game does just this. Festivals are held all over the country and, thanks to the generous sponsorship of Esso, even the smallest primary school has a chance to get to the finals, played on a County ground.

Wrigley Softball

We are told that the supremacy of West Indian cricket owes much to the fact that boys play softball cricket. In this country the Wrigley company is helping to introduce the game in schools which have little or no facilities, since it requires a minimum of equipment and can be played anywhere. Here again every schoolboy and girl has a chance to be in one of the sixteen teams which travel to Edgbaston each year for the finals.

The Need for More Cricket

We do not agree with the Minister for Sport, who talks of the demise of cricket in state schools. Nevertheless we are sad that so many schools, particularly in the comprehensive area, do not play cricket. It is our task to improve the situation as we feel that no games programme can be complete if our national summer game is not played. We are particularly distressed at the steady deterioration in the upkeep of many school grounds. An in-depth study in Norfolk last year showed how the situation can be improved even under the present financial limitations. We also support the provision of more non-turf wickets.

Coaching

ESCA is particularly indebted to the National Coaching Scheme, under the the guidance of the National Coach, Keith Andrew, and his team of coaches. They work enthusiastically at schools all over the country, and this can only be beneficial. The sponsorship of the National Westminster Bank for the Proficiency Award Scheme is ensuring that thousands of young cricketers commence playing in the right way.

The Clubs

A far-reaching scheme has been started by the Trustee Savings Bank to enable school leavers to join clubs. Go into any Trustee Savings Bank and they will let you have a booklet telling you all about the scheme. We are cooperating with the NCA, because we believe in the values of the game.

A Final Message to You

If you go to a cricket-playing school, keep on playing the game for enjoyment. If you go to a school which does not play cricket, why not try to do something about it? When you leave school – or even before – join a club in your area.

Remember that 'cricket is endless in its appeal to those who love it and understand it.'

THE LORD'S TAVERNERS CRICKETER COLTS TROPHY 1984

It was probably inevitable that when the Lord's Taverners, *The Cricketer* and ESCA got together to think up a cricket competition it would turn out to be not only the largest, but the longest, in the world. The competition is sponsored by the Lord's Taverners, and administered by ESCA and *The Cricketer*, and is based on the Schools County Associations. Each County runs a knock-out competition at Under 14 level one season to provide a team to represent it in the National competition in the following season at Under 15 level. So when over 1,600 schools begin to play their matches in April, it is not until sixteen months later that the final is played. A long trek indeed, but one which is having a tremendous influence on the game in schools.

Only three previous winners won through to represent their counties, so it was odds-on that a new winner would emerge this year. In the Midlands, Shrewsbury carried all before them in the first four rounds, defeating Dolgellau, Wolverhampton, Rugby and Nottingham High School in turn. At the same time Arnold School from Blackpool were winning their way to the semi-final steadily. In a high-scoring semi-final Arnold beat Shrewsbury by 5 runs. In the other half of the draw, the fancied schools, Sherborne, Cheltenham, Radley and Tonbridge got through to the Fourth Round, and Cheltenham proved to be the strongest.

Once again all roads led to Edgbaston on 10 July – the Warwickshire County Cricket Club are true friends of ESCA – and an exciting match was forecast. Cheltenham started steadily, but it was not until Harris and Davies got together for the third wicket that we saw what excellent cricket this competition produces. They put on 103 for this wicket, and when Harris was caught off the bowling of Halsall, Davies was joined by St. J. Large, and another 47 were quickly added. At the end of the 40 overs Cheltenham had reached 205 with only 5 wickets down.

Schoolboys always find it difficult to pace an innings against such a large total, and although Arnold batted steadily, they could not score quickly enough, and began to lose quick wickets in their search for runs. When Hampshire mopped up the tail with 4 wickets for 9 runs in 8 overs, Cheltenham had won by over 100 runs.

In presenting the awards, and the *Cricketer* Cup, Capt J. A. R. Swainson, the Director of the Lord's Taverners, who have sponsored the competition for over ten years, paid tribute to the skill and enthusiasm of the players and looked forward to another great season in 1985, the teams for which are already being decided all over the country in the County Competitions.

WINNERS

1972 King Edward VIth School, Morpeth
1973 Winchester College
1974 Radley College
1975 Radley College
1976 Stamford School
1977 Radley College
1978 Queen Elizabeth G.S. Blackburn
1979 Tonbridge School
1980 Bedford Modern School
1981 Peterlee Howletch School
1982 Taunton School
1983 Queen's College, Taunton
1984 Cheltenham College

Cheltenham College jubilant in victory.

LORD'S TAVERNERS CRICKETER COLTS TROPHY FINAL 1984

CHELTENHAM COLLEGE

A. D. L. Thomas ...	c Jones b MacGregor	19
D. J. W. Hampshire .	lbw b Jones	12
C. M. Harris	c Poole b Halsall	47
O. G. Davies	not out	64
S. R. St J. Large	b McFarlane	33
J. Alwyn	b MacFarlane	4
R. T. Davies	not out	1
C. H. Millward		
A. C. McAllester ...	} did not bat	
S. D. Lane		
H. A. Wynne		
	Extras	25
(40 overs)**Total** (for 5 wkts)		205

BOWLING	O	M	R	W
Johnson	8	0	41	0
MacGregor	8	2	22	1
Jones	8	1	34	1
Halsall	8	0	46	1
McFarlane	82	0	37	2

ARNOLD SCHOOL

J. M. Muir	lbw b Davies, O.	11
M. A. Johnson	b Large	17
R. G. Halsall	lbw b Large	1
J. A. N. McFarlane	b Large	12
A. D. Jones	b Hampshire	1
P. S. Smith	c McAllester b Hampshire	0
G. S. Poole	lbw b Davies, O.	9
G. A. Guy	b Harris	0
R. W. Brooks	c Davies, O. b Hampshire	14
A. J. McGregor	b Hampshire	7
R. J. Geddes	not out	2
	Extras	8
Total		82

BOWLING	O	M	R	W
Davies, O.	5	1	14	2
Harris	4.5	1	15	1
Large	8	0	36	3
Hampshire	8	4	9	4

Cheltenham College won by 123 runs

THE LORD'S TAVERNERS CRICKETER
COLTS TROPHY
1984 NATIONAL ROUNDS

First Round

Wolverhampton G.S.	95–1	Rydal School	92–9
Shrewsbury School	204–0	Ysgol Y Gader, Dolgellau	84
The Minster, Leominster	49	Rugby School	249–2
R.G.S. Worcester	157–4	Lutterworth	126
Caister, Lincoln	36	Nottingham H.S.	37–6
Perse School	138	Charles Burrell, Norwich	130
Bedford Modern	45–1	Kimbolton (rain)	92
Hirst, Ashington	73	Queen Elizabeth, Penrith	77–2
Stockport School	173–9	Bydales School, Redcar	173–8
Sherborne School	96–4	King Edward's, Southampton	94
Blundell's School, Tiverton	185–7	Mullion School, Cornwall	184–6
Beechen Cliff School, Bath	132	Cheltenham College	146
St. Teilo's, Cardiff	129–9	Bassaleg, Gwent	143–7
Cefn Hengoed, W. Glam.	76	Brynteg, Bridgend	94
Caterham H.S., Ilford	107–5	Woodbridge school	106
Radley College	165–1	Dr. Challoner's G.S. Amersham	163–3
John Roan, London	109	Wellington College	252–3

Second Round

Wolverhampton G.S.	154	Shrewsbury School	165–9
Rugby School	136	R.G.S. Worcester	51
Nottingham H.S.	181–6	Perse School	49
Bedford Modern School	148–2	Oundle School	144–9
Bydales School	64	Repton School	124–8
Durham School	148	Pocklington School	178–8
Arnold School	90–3	Wirral G.S.	86
Queen Elizabeth's, Penrith	121	Batley G.S.	138–7
		Marlborough College	158–6
Sherborne School	162–4	Castle School, Taunton	172
Blundell's School	173–9	Bassaleg	scr.
Cheltenham College	w.o.	Ysgol Y Strade, Llanelli	136
Brynteg School	97	Tonbridge School	178–3
Caterham H.S.	95	Wimbledon College	91
Hurstpierpoint, Sussex	151	Radley College	113–5
Enfield G.S.	109	Verulam School, St. Albans	73
Wellington College	74–2		

Third Round

Shrewsbury School	142–1	Rugby School	138–6
Nottingham H.S.	99–6	Bedford Modern School	95
Repton School	87	Pocklington School	137–9
Arnold School	116–1	Batley G.S.	114–8
Sherborne School	126–8	Blundell's School	90
Cheltenham College	36–3	Ysgol Y Strade	32
Tonbridge School	153–6	Hurstpierpoint School	149–8
Radley College	218	Wellington College	211

Fourth Round

Shrewsbury School	121–4	Nottingham H.S.	121–9
Pocklington School	92	Arnold School	93–5
Sherborne School	119–9	Cheltenham College	120–4
Tonbridge School	117	Radley College	121–6

Semi-Finals

Arnold School	196	Shrewsbury School	191
Cheltenham College	159	Radley College	134

Final

Cheltenham College	205–5	Arnold School	82

MILLFIELD WIN THE BARCLAYS BANK SCHOOLS CUP

Under 17 Winners Millfield
Standing: M. D. Golding, H. J.
Bennett, J. M. A. Biggs,
A. R. Phillips,
P. J. Stephenson,
D. J. Luckes, I. A. Duncan,
H. R. J. Trump.
Kneeling: A. C. H. Seymour,
M. T. Parkinson, R. W. Hill
(captain), J. C. M. Atkinson,
D. J. Nirmalalingham.

No less than 480 schools set out in this Under 17 competition organised in conjunction with the English Schools Cricket Association, entry being open to all schools and colleges affiliated to a County Schools Cricket Association. All boys playing in the competition must have been under seventeen years of age on 31 August 1983. Organised on a regional basis, this 45 overs-a-side competition staged four regional finals; North, Midlands, South and West, and the four regional winners met in the semi-finals at Barclays Sports Ground at Ealing on Monday 9 July. The winning teams were Abbot Beyne, who beat Durham by 3 wickets, and Millfield who beat Lord Williams', Thame by 90 runs.

Abbot Beyne and Millfield met in the Cup Final the next day, this time at Barclays other ground at Norbury. Millfield, unbeaten in school matches this season and having a side which one or two people who should know consider to be one of their best ever, were strong favourites; but they were soon in trouble: half the side was out for little more than 50. Were Abbot Beyne on the fringe of a famous victory? They were not! Trump and Stephenson got things together, and Trump batted to the end of the 45 overs undefeated with 88, and the obvious match winner. Stephenson was an admirable foil in the partnership worth just short of 100. Trump, under fifteen, and with three more years to go at Millfield, batted with great composure. Yet it is said that he is more likely to make his name with his off-spin bowling. They might, perhaps, have included his fielding in this assessment: hc held a fine catch, and with a wonderful pick-up and throw hit the stumps with only one to aim at for the vital running out of J. Emery, who was going well at the time.

Rhodes played a commendably courageous innings for Abbot Beyne; in fact he alone could cope with Millfield's varied attack, scoring 64 not out. The next highest score in Abbot Beyne's innings was extras, 20. Parkinson took 3 for 22 (watched by his distinguished father, Michael Parkinson), and Hill 3 for 38, the latter apparently not being an accredited front-line bowler, and was used as the fifth bowler because five had to bowl in a 45 over match. As he failed to score his three wickets were no doubt an unexpected and very enjoyable bonus for him.

This was a game of cricket which would have encouraged followers of the game who are disappointed with things at the top level. It had a triumvirate of virtues: no helmets, no noisy rowdies, and sportsmanship of the highest order.

Millfield had three times reached their regional final but only this third year getting to the final, and so they now join Bablake and Monmouth as competition winners. When Bablake won in 1982, the first year of the competition, 270 schools had entered.

Now numbers have reached 480. The administration involved in accepting many more may well make it too difficult – enough is enough. Certainly in a very short space of time the competition has established itself as something schools are very keen to enter, and even more keen to win! Barclays sponsorship and ESCA's organising ability has proved a partnership of immense value to cricket.

Robert Hill, captain of Millfield School's Under 17 team, receiving the Barclays Bank Schools Cricket Cup from Henry Lambert, Chairman of Barclays Bank UK.

BARCLAYS BANK UNDER 17 FINAL

ABBOT BEYNE v MILLFIELD
at Barclays Bank Ground, Norbury, 10 July, 1984

MILLFIELD

A. Seymour	c Bladon b Emery, J.	17
A. Phillips	b Clarke	2
J. Atkinson	b Emery, J.	22
R. Hill	c Ali b Emery, J.	0
D. Nirmalalingan	c Godfrey b Ali	9
H. Trump	not out	88
P. Stephenson	c and b Rhodes	33
D. Luckes	c Drew b Rhodes	16
H. Bennett	not out	0
I. Duncan	} did not bat	
M. Parkinson		
	Extras (6b, 3lb, 2w, 5nb)	16

(45 overs) **Total** (for 7 wkts) 203

BOWLING	O	M	R	W
Clarke	10	3	45	1
Emery, J.	10	1	36	3
Ali	6	0	31	1
Rhodes	10	1	45	2
Rowley	7	0	20	0
Orme	2	0	10	0

ABBOT BEYNE

J. Rowley	st Duncan b Parkinson	13
R. Bladon	c Trump b Parkinson	0
J. Emery	run out	17
N. Rhodes	not out	64
A. Ali	b Hill	1
R. Emery	st Duncan b Stephenson	1
K. Godfrey	b Hill	2
J. Orme	b Hill	6
C. Colley	b Parkinson	1
G. Drew	c Phillips b Parkinson	7
E. Clarke	did not bat	
	Extras (3b, 7lb, 5w, 5nb)	20

(9 wickets) (45 overs) **Total** 132

BOWLING	O	M	R	W
Parkinson	10	4	22	3
Atkinson	8	2	20	0
Trump	7	0	17	0
Stephenson	10	4	15	2
Hill	10	2	38	3

Millfield won by 71 runs

THE WRIGLEY SOFTBALL CRICKET FINALS 1984

A great spot to be on 11 July was the car park at Edgbaston. From ten o'clock onwards, a series of coaches, minibuses and cars disgorged 160 ten-year old cricketers from sixteen schools, together with their teachers and parents. The boys tumbled out of their vehicles, clutching their brand-new colourful Wrigley cricket-bags, and hurried as fast as they could to look at the Test Ground, where they were to play. As they arrived in their dressing rooms, each team was given distinctive headgear, and the boys and girls quickly changed to get ready for the fray. These teams had won their Area competition, and their own County competition before this, and they came from places as far afield as Glasgow and Devon.

What is the attraction of this game of softball

which is now played in so many schools? It is a game which is fun to play, and safe to play. Because it can be played on any surface, it is encouraging cricket among youngsters, not only in this country, but also in such places as India, Malaysia and Australia.

In each game, on a fifteen yard pitch, a team of eight players bat in pairs for three overs each. If a player is dismissed, he does not leave the field, but stays there to bat on. Every dismissal means that 6 runs are deductd from the starting score of 200, so it doesn't pay to get out too many times. No bowler is allowed to bowl more than three overs. And of course the team that wins is the one with the most runs at the end: a short, exciting game, in which every player takes a full share.

This year we used the main arena (four games at a time) and the Colts Pitch (two games at a time), and the sixteen teams were divided up into four leagues to decide the ultimate semi-finalists. Last Year's winners, Ovingham from Northumberland, were there, but they quickly found that they were'nt going to win again. Play began at 11.am. and when the final was reached at 6 o'clock, I don't know whether the players or the spectators were the more exhausted!

Part of the group of 160 under eleven-year-olds who played in the finals of the Wrigley Softball Cricket Trophy on the Warwickshire C.C. ground at Edgbaston on 12 July, 1984.

Area Winners:

Scotland: Hyndland Primary School, Glasgow
North West: Arnot C.P. School, Walton, Liverpool
South: Burlington Junior School, New Malden
West Midlands: Whitchurch C. of E. Junior School, Shropshire
North: Ovingham C.P. School, Prudhoe, Northumberland
S W Midlands: Ridgeway School, Redditch, Worcester
South Midlands: Dunmore Junior School, Abingdon
South East: Portway Junior School, Plistow, London, E13
North East: Chiveley Park, Belmont, Durham
West: Tavistock Primary School, Devon
West Midlands: Kingswell Junior School, Arnold, Nottingham
South Wales: Bishopston Junior School, Swansea
Yorkshire and Humberside: Messingham School, Scunthorpe
London: De Beauvoir School, Hackney
Midlands: City Road Junior, Birmingham
North Wales: Ysgol Maesydre, Welshpool

* At the end of the Group Matches, the positions were:

		Pts			Pts
A	Arnot	6	B	Ridgeway	6
	Hyndland	2		Ovingham	2
	Burlington	2		Dunmore	2
	Whitchurch	2		Portway	0

		Pts			Pts
C	Kingswell	4	D	Maesydre	6
	Belmont	4		Messingham	4
	Bishopston	2		City Rd	2
	Tavistock	2		De Beauvoir	0

Having won their Groups, all four semi-finalists were no mean performers. Arnot were due to play Kingswell – who had got through because they had beaten Belmont who had as many points as they had – while Maesydre had to play Ridgeway. Arnot, who had looked a thoroughly efficient side all day, proved much too strong for Kingswell, while on the adjacent pitch Maesydre outplayed Ridgeway. The scores were: Kingswell 183; Arnot 259; Maesydre 213; Ridgeway 163.

It was a great final, but the expertise of the Liverpudlians took their total to 237, and although Maesydre scored plenty of runs, they also achieved too many dismissals, and finished on 210.

A very interested spectator was Brian Johnston, who came along at the invitation of Trevor Bailey, who had been responsible for initiating the competition. He presented every boy with a plaque before the semi-finals, and at the end handed over the Wrigley Cup to the Arnot captain, who displayed it in true Liverpool style. Brian Johnston expressed his enthusiasm in his usual way with his own inimitable jokes.

The English Schools Cricket Association has been proud to be able to incorporate this tournament in their overall plan for the future, and is grateful to Wrigley for making it financially possible.

Raising the standard
By Trevor Bailey

The Wrigley Softball Cricket Trophy 1984. Brian Johnston, who presented the awards, and Trevor Bailey with Arnot County Primary School team from Walton, Liverpool, who defeated Maesydre School, Welshpool, in the final.

The main objectives of softball cricket are to provide a game which is fun, safe and can be played almost anywhere and to encourage cricket at primary school level. In addition, I believe it is such a good game that it will spread, increase interest and raise the overall standard.

I am delighted that these things are already occurring. Softball cricket is now being played in India, and I've been told of a particularly interesting success story following its introduction here.

In 1981 Feniscowes School, a small county primary in Blackburn, entered the Wrigley Softball Tournament and won the North West of England section, which earned them a place in the finals at Edgbaston. Although they did not win, their performance was noted by their local Cherry Tree Cricket Club. Showing commendable sense and imagination, the club offered all eight boys free membership for a year, which six accepted.

The six became members of the club's under 13 side, which went on to win the Lancashire Club Cricket competition in 1983. They also just failed to qualify for the All England finals when they lost to a Wolverhampton team which included five county players. In sharp contrast, six of the Cherry Tree side came from one small primary school and lived within two miles of the club!

Six of the Cherry Tree lads had already been

chosen for the town team in 1982 and two were selected for Lancashire and given county caps – not bad considering only three were awarded. They are currently undergoing trials for the county. Another two members of that original Feniscowes team are currently playing for East Lancashire CC.

This illustrates that those 1981 finals at Edgbaston did nore than just provide the participants with a memorable day. It helped to set them on the right road. My hope is that the players in the sixteen teams at Edgbaston in 1984 will experience similar benefits. Possibly one may return to this ground as a Test player in ten years' time, but more important is that all 160 carry on enjoying a very special game.

The Rules
In Softball Cricket the laws of cricket shall apply and N.C.A. recommendations for junior cricket should be observed.

1 Each team shall be comprised of 8 players.
2 The length of the pitch shall be 15 yards
3 Junior indoor cricket stumps should be used when possible. If not available, any suitable alternative may be used at the dscretion of the organiser.
4 Each game shall consist on one innings per team, each innings to be 12 (6 ball) overs' duration (16 overs when time permits).
5 The batting side shall be divided into pairs, each pair batting for 3 overs (4 overs when playing a 16 overs per side game) and changing at the end of the third, sixth and ninth overs (again, in the 16 over game at the end of the fourth, eighth and twelfth over).
6 No player on the fielding side may bowl more than 3 overs (4 overs in the 16 overs per side game). The wicket-keeper may not bowl.
7 Each team shall commence batting with a team score of 200 runs.
8 Each time a wicket falls, 6 runs must be deducted from the team score.
9 When a batsman is dismissed, he should immediately change ends with the non striker (on all but the last ball of the over).
10 Unless specified in local rules a normal (preferably worn) tennis ball should be used as the match ball.

EXCITING COMPETITIONS

AND THE VITAL ROLE PLAYED BY THE NATIONAL CRICKET ASSOCIATION

The National Cricket Association was founded in 1968 broadly to look after recreational and youth cricket, as well as coaching. In their offices at Lord's, which are above the England Dressing Room and overlooking the most famous of all grounds, they run the cricket competitions and organise the coaching courses that encourage many youngsters to play cricket at an early age, introducing them to a game that will give them enjoyment for the rest of their lives.

Peter Sutcliffe, who was NCA's first Director of Coaching, considered that the trend away from cricket at schools could benefit Clubs so in the early 1970's a pilot scheme for a completely new cricket competition took place. The Lord's Taverners, those great benefactors of cricket, financed the venture and the competition was for Under 13-year-olds. Everyone who has played cricket at school can remember spending the match watching others perform because they had either got a low score or were making up the team and batting low in the order, thereby not deriving a great deal of enjoyment from the game. It was this problem that Peter Sutcliffe was anxious to overcome and he came up with a revolutionary new idea which would guarantee all players total participation. Each team would consist of eight players; they would bat in pairs and all except the wicket-keeper would bowl. In a twenty over match each pair would bat for five overs, and when they lost their wicket they did not go out; instead the wickets lost at the end of the innings were divided into the total to give an average. Keith Andrew, the present NCA Director of Coaching has introduced a more simple scoring method: each team commences its innings with a score of 200 runs and loses 8 runs for each wicket lost; of course runs are scored and added to the total.

The Under 13 8-a-side cricket soon became popular after the initial pilot competition in

1972. When it went national in 1973 each county ran a competition and their winner went to a Regional Final and the eight Regional Final winners went forward to the National Finals. In the first three years the Finals were held in Birmingham. 1976 saw a change of venue to Lancing College in Sussex where as before a girls team were involved. 1977 again saw a change of venue to Sherborne School in Dorset where they have been held ever since.

The Finals week must be a great experience for all the young cricketers. Each team plays the other seven finalists with games taking place in the morning and afternoon on a large field in the picturesque Dorset countryside which can accommodate all four matches within sight of each other. The evenings are taken up with film shows, quizzes and talks on umpiring: a great week in the cricket education of any youngster. The eight umpires who stand throughout the week are appointed by the Association of cricket umpires, and there is a waiting list of over thirty who want to be involved at Sherborne. The standard of sportsmanship is excellent, the fielding is of a high quality and there are always some very green flannels.

Since 1972 when the competition was introduced the number of teams playing has increased to approximately 1,000. All the teams now play for a magnificent trophy presented in honour of the great England batsman Ken Barrington. NatWest Bank sponsor the whole tournament in conjunction with the National Cricket Association and the Lord's Taverners.

WINNERS

1972	Clayhall	(Essex)
1973	Clifton	(Lancashire)
1974	Old Esthameians	(Essex)
1975	Snaresbrook	(Essex)
1976	Brondesbury	(Middlesex)
1977	St. James's	(Sussex)
1978	Marske	(Yorkshire)
1979	Preston Nomads	(Sussex)
1980	Clayhall	(Essex)
1981	Wem	(Shropshire)
1982	Taunton	(Somerset)
1983	Wanstead	(Essex)
1984	Sheffield Collegiate	(Yorkshire)

Having intoduced an Under 13 competition it was not long before there were requests for additional competitions for different age groups. However, it was not until 1977 that the Under 15 Club Cricket Championship was introduced, again with the financial help of the Lord's Taverners.

The format of the new competition was different from that used in the Ken Barrington Cup; it was decided to keep to the normal game of cricket, and each team batted for 20 overs with no boy allowed to bowl more than 4 overs. Each County Cricket Association arranged an internal championship and their winners went forward to county play-offs; then the sixteen winners then went to four Regional Finals with those winners making it to the National Finals. The first year saw the finals at Trent Bridge, giving some lucky boys the chance to play on a Test Match ground; unfortunately it rained and the games had to be hastily re-arranged. The following year saw Trent Bridge again as the venue for the finals, with Leicestershire CC hosting the event in 1979 and 1980.

It is not perhaps so strange that young cricketers should take a long time to bowl their overs, but the fact that they do determined a move for the finals to Moseley Cricket Club where two semi-finals could take place simultaneously, avoiding the need for a very late

Under 15 Club Championship Winners, Long Eaton. Standing: J. Jordison (Team Manager), T. Deas, B. Shepherd, J. Morris, J. Barry, C. Smith, N. Daykin, B. Howden, J. Daykin (Asst. Team Manager). Kneeling: P. Carver, M. Simnett, I. Hopkins, M. Harrison (Captain), P. Harrison, M. Allen.

final. At Trent Bridge the Nottingham Forest floodlights were nearly needed as the boys never exceeded 14 overs and hour! The Harry Secombe cup is the trophy played for, and 1983 saw the first year of the Under 15 Club Cricket Championship being sponsored by Debenham Tewson & Chinnocks, a firm of International Real Estate Consultants and chartered Surveyors.

WINNERS

1977:	Dunlop CC	(Warwickshire)
1978:	Brondesbury CC	(Middlesex)
1979:	Loughborough	
	Carillon CC	(Leicestershire)
1980:	Bradfield CC	(Yorkshire)
1981:	Chelmsford CC	(Essex)
1982:	Taunton CC	(Somerset)
1983	Long Eaton CC	(Nottinghamshire)

With the establishment of two club-based junior competitions it was logical to extend the programme and introduce a County Competition. Much debate centred on the right age group for such a competition and it was eventually decided to have an Under 16 County Championship. Sponsorship was essential for such a competition, and Commercial Union Assurance willingly provided the necessary funds.

1979 saw the first Championship and now there are eight groups where each team plays the others and the group winners go into a quarter-final. The system is very similar to the Benson & Hedges Cup in first class cricket until the semi-finals and final, when the four teams gather at Uppingham School for three days where they play each team to determine the champions.

This competition provides the best standard of youth cricket at Under 16 level. Many players since 1979 have progressed to the staff of their County Cricket Club and who knows someone may soon play for England. Some already have, playing for England Young Cricketers.

The first winners were Middlesex, with a team comprising of players who had played in the Under 13 and Under 15 Competitions. It must surely prove that the system is working for the benefit of young cricketers.

1984 sees a change of sponsor with Texaco, sponsors of one-day internationals, taking over.

WINNERS

1979:	Middlesex
1980:	Somerset
1981:	Hampshire
1982:	Lancashire
1983:	Yorkshire
1984:	Lancashire

NCA Under 16 County
Championship Winners 1983,
Yorkshire.
Standing: C. Smith (Youth
Organiser), J. Spence,
B. Crabtree, M. Robinson,
G. Liley, A. Reaks, J. Firth,
D. Batty (Team Manager).
Sitting: P. Berry, A. Bethel,
R. Blakey, G. Duggan,
J. Swain, C. Nichols, A. Hugill.

English Schools Course, Crystal Place N.R.C., April 1984
Back row: John Wake (NCA Staff Coach), Graham Saville (Chief Coach, NCA National Coach), David Baines (Easingwold School, Yorkshire), Michael Roseberry (Durham), Nigel Cheeseright (Wetherby H.S., Yorkshire), Nick Speak (Parrs Wood H.S., Lancashire), Andrew Goldsmith (Sleaford College, Surrey), Mark Robinson (Hull G.S., Humberside), Matthew Jacob (NE Surrey Tech., Surrey), Andrew Parker (Isle Sixth Form College, Wisbech), Daniel Kelleher (Erith College of Tech., Kent), Martin Roberts (Helston School,

Cornwall), Stephen Heath (King Edward VI, Birmingham), Nick Willetts (King Edward VI, Birmingham), Paul Bail (Millfield, Somerset), Robert Thomas (Eaglesfield, London), Tony Barrington (NCA Staff Coach), Ken Inghan (NCA Staff Coach, ESCA U-19 Team Manager). Front row: Nick Pringle (Taunton, Somerset), David Billington (Kirkbie Kendal, Cumbria), John Kershaw (Bacup & Rawtenstall G.S., Lancashire), Paul Vincent (Dean Close, Gloucestershire), Ian Redpath (Barstable, Essex), Mark O'Connor (King Edward, Southampton, Hampshire), Andrew Platts (Chesterfield Tech., Derbyshire), Chris Mays (Lancing, Sussex), Jon Sheppard (Hampton School, Middlesex).

FIVE YOUNG CRICKETERS
OF THE YEAR
In alphabetical order

NEIL LENHAM
Brighton College

Neil was born in Worthing on 17 December, 1965 and educated at
Broadwater Manor Preparatory School and Brighton College.

Up to date he has made forty-two centuries, which includes two double
centuries, with a highest score of 223 not out. He played his first game for
Sussex 2nd XI at the age of fourteen against Surrey 2nd XI, making top
score in the Sussex second innings.

Playing for ESCA Under 15s he topped 50 in his four innings, making a
century against Scotland. He captained ESCA Under 15s, and played a total
of six innings in all for the ESCA Under 15, topping 50 on five occasions. At
the age of sixteen he led the Sussex 2nd XI batting averages, scoring over
500 runs during his school summer holiday, with a top score of 123 not out
against Essex 2nd XI at Eastbourne.

During the 1983 season he played in the last two of a three match Test
series against the Australian Under 19s, heading the England batting
averages. He played for ESCA Under 19s in 1983 against the Australians
and Scotland, scoring runs in all his innings, and represented MCC Schools
against N.A.Y.C. at Lord's, scoring 30 and 60.

In 1984 Neil totalled 1,534 runs for Brighton College in the public school
season; more runs in public schools cricket than any other schoolboy
batsman since 1945. His overall total of 4,084 runs in first eleven cricket is
the highest total ever recorded by a batsman at Brighton College. He also
took 118 wickets in his first eleven career. Neil joined the Sussex
professional staff in July 1984.

He also plays for Sussex Under 19s at hockey, and squash for the College
first team.

CHRIS MAYS
Lancing

Born in Brighton on 11 May 1966, Chris has been playing cricket since the age of five. This was when he first came under the influence of Pat Cale, now Assistant County Coach, but then on the staff of St. Christopher's School, Hove. Here he was responsible for the early development of Chris's cricket. Moving on to Lancing College, he immediately won his place in the first eleven, in which he has played for five years, watched over by the cricket master, Alan Evan-Jones.

An aggressive opening bat and an off-spinner of high quality, he has had some outstanding performances at Lancing. He took a record number of wickets in 1982: 58. This season he has excelled himself with a total of 737 runs for the school with an average of 43 and with seven 50s. He scored 99 v Epsom School, and took 6 for 70 v Tonbridge and 5 for 36 v MCC.

He won his Under 15 England Schools cap in 1982. This year he has won his place in the England Schools Under 19 team. On the way he has taken 7 for 22 v ESCA West, 4 wickets for 34 for the HMC Schools v ESCA, and 6 for 89 for ESCA v NAYC, and finally 2 wickets for the NCA XI in the one-day game v Combined Services.

On the club scene he has played for Sussex Young Cricketers in the Cambridge Festival. He plays for Cryptics St. Mary's C.C., and to date in six matches has taken 30 wickets at a cost of 6 each, taking 8 for 16 against Ringmer and scoring 98 v Ditchling.

This year he has played three times for Sussex 2nd XI, scoring 100* v Surrey 2nd XI, and three times for the Under 25s, taking 3 for 15 against Hampshire.

Chris enjoys his cricket, and also takes it seriously as his record shows. An all-rounder of great promise, he could eventually play a vital part in the Test arena.

MICHAEL ROSEBERRY
Durham School

Michael, an outstanding attacking batsman with a full range of strokes, has shown enormous potential from a very early age progressing through the Durham Under 11s, 13s and 15s to the English Schools North team and the English Schools Under 15 team in 1982, scoring 129 against Wales. His awards during this season included the Lord's Taverners MCC Cricketer of the Year award, the *Sun* newspaper Cricketer of the Year and the Cricket Society Wetherall award for the best all rounder in HMC Schools. He is a change bowler of medium pace who gets among the wickets each time he bowls, once taking 7 for 46 for Durham against Giggleswick.

The year 1984 has been a natural progression for him. He scored the highest total of runs ever scored in a season at Durham School – in excess of 1,300 – he has hit ten centuries, one of them when Captain of MCC Schools against the National Association of Young Cricketers at Lord's, and he was made Captain of the English Schools Under 19 team.

In 1983 he hit a double century for Durham against St. Bees – 216 – and took Durham to the final of the Lord's Taverners Cricketer Colts Trophy when they were beaten by Taunton. Not surprisingly, a number of first-class Counties are watching his progress very carefully and he has already played for Glamorgan Under 19, and Northamptonshire and Warwickshire second Elevens. But he still has another year at school as he is not eighteen until 28 November 1984. Two of his centuries this summer were for Sunderland in the Durham County League – 109 not out against Billingham, and 107 not out against Boldon. Michael, a great thinker about the game of cricket, is held in high regard as a Captain. His future in whatever direction he wants it to take is assured.

HARVEY TRUMP
Millfield

Harvey will never forget July 1984. At the beginning of the month, he was in the Millfield Under 17 team which won the Barclays Bank Cup, ensuring victory with a magnificent 88 not out. In late July, he was selected to captain the West in the United Friendly Festival in Hull. He led them to the Championship, scoring 67 v North and 43 v Midlands. He was then asked to lead ESCA against the President's XI in the two-day match. In the second innings they collapsed against his accurate off-spin bowling (He took 6 for 25) and ESCA won. Immediately afterwards he was chosen as captain of England against Wales and Scotland. What a month!

He is an all-rounder to be reckoned with, excelling in his own age-group, and also playing for most of the season for Millfield 1st XI, giving him a cricket maturity well beyond his years. Technically very sound, he plays the bowling on its merits and seems unflappable when at the wicket. He hits the ball beautifully in front of square-leg.

A Somerset boy, born on 11 October 1968, he learnt his early cricket at Edgarley School, where he captained the Under 11, Under 12 and Under 13 teams. He particularly remembers scoring 126 against Wells Cathedral School.

Harvey has played for the Somerset Under 15 team for three years, scoring many runs and taking many wickets. As years go by, his successes continue – one outstanding day scoring 123 and taking 7 for 42 against Clifton Under 16s.

He is a front line bowler, and has had to learn in his captaincy when to bowl and when not to bowl. He certainly knew when to bowl at Hull! He is an off-spinner with good control of line and length with subtle variation of pace, and he likes to give the ball plenty of air.

TREVOR WARD
Hextable School, Dartford

Trevor, born on 18 January 1968, and attending Hextable School in Dartford, Kent, is a very positive character, who never tires of making runs – a modern Bradman!

It is encouraging that he first came to the notice of the experts with his tremendous aggressive fielding, which he displayed for two years as an England Schools Under 15 player, and this year as an Under 19 player for England.

In 1983 he showed us the shape of things to come by winning the Neil Lloyd Shield at the United Friendly Festival in Surrey, among his scores being 116 against the Midlands. This followed some aggressive play in 1982.

In the same year he once scored 471 runs in three days, playing for his school against King's, Canterbury and Harvey, Folkestone, and for Kent Schools v Berkshire.

Here are some of his successes in 1984:
Barclay's Bank Cup (Playing for Hextable): 132* v Chatham House, Ramsgate, 122 v Colfe's, 155* v Rutlish, 67 v Lord William's Thame (South Final).

For Dartford C.C. 1st XI in the Kent League: Total runs 624 at an average of 41.63, with a highest score of 118 v Brentwood, Essex.

He plays for Colin Page's Kent County Colts most Sundays.

He was chosen as a squad member of the Association of Kent Cricket Clubs for the Under 19 Festival.

After scoring 59 out of 167 for an ESCA XI against Middlesex 2nd XI, he played for ESCA against the HMC and subsequently for the MCC Schools v NAYC.

As he hopes to take up cricket as a career, his future will be watched with great interest. The ESCA Handbook records that he is the hardest hitter seen in schools cricket at Under 15 level since Mike Gatting in 1972.

THE YOUNG CRICKETER CLUB
Run by *The Cricketer* International Magazine

For the £2 annual fee, the young cricketer receives the following immediate benefits:

* 10% off all Stuart Surridge equipment and cricket at nearly 100 well known sports shops;
* 5% off new junior membership fee of Lancashire, Middlesex, Gloucestershire, Sussex, Worcestershire, Warwickshire, Northamptonshire and Glamorgan, with other benefits being negotiated with the remaining county clubs for 1985;
* 5% off several Young Activity holidays;
* 5% off all items in *The Cricketer* shop;
* 10% off coaching at Alf Gover's world famous indoor cricket school in London and a price reduction at many other coaching courses at other indoor centres;
* a special personalised YOUNG CRICKETER MEMBERSHIP CARD;
* a special offer on a subscription to *The Cricketer* for new subscribers – 12 issues for £9.40;
* 5% off some of the superb holidays organised by *The Cricketer*.

Having established a large core of members, there is no limit to the potential sphere of the Club's activities – trips to Test matches or one-day finals, a special Club cricket weekend tournament, coaching courses for Club members, further discounts on books and equipment and, eventually, a separate newsletter for members supplementing news already published in *The Cricketer* magazine.

Small boy to rest of team: 'Come on, lads, only two quid to join the Young Cricketer club. Then we can get money off one of them Stuart Surridge jumbo bats!' (With apologies to *Punch*).

For the young cricket lover, because he does not have to be a brilliant player himself, this club fills an important vacuum. There are, obviously, local cricket clubs which a youngster can join to play and, possibly, talk about the game; but there is no national club for the young cricketer – and hatis what the YCC is aiming to become.

The Club is still in its infancy and its future success depends not only on the cooperation and cotinued support of people in the game, but on the young cricketers themselves: it is their club. *The Cricketer* hopes to encourage more to join the Club and then to nurture and an interest in and enthusiasm for all aspects of the game which, hopefully, will be maintained well beyond the age when they leave the Young Cricketer Club.

If you would like to join the Young Cricketer Club, just write to *The Cricketer* at Beach Hanger, Ashurst, Tunbridge Wells, Kent TN3 9ST GIVING YOUR DATE OF BIRTH AND NAME OF SCHOOL AND ENCLOSING YOUR £2 MEMBERSHIP FEE, and you will receive the details of the club and your own personal membership card like the one published on this page.

YOUNG CRICKETER CLUB

MEMBERSHIP

№ 527

Name

Address

Date of Birth

Not transferable. Valid until 30th April 198

THE UNITED FRIENDLY INSURANCE SCHOOLS CRICKET FESTIVAL

For the last sixteen years, the culminating event of the ESCA County programme has been the Under 15 Cricket Festival of Regional Matches followed by the annual match against the President's XI. For the past four years this has all been made possible by the generous sponsorship of the United Friendly Insurance Company. There are over 250 Inter-County games played at this level, and from these the outstanding boys are chosen to represent their Regions in the Festival, this year held in Hull and organised by the Humberside Schools C.A. led by Ken Lake.

The Regional squads were:

NORTH: R. Gofton (Humberside) Capt, G. barker, K. Krikkin (wkp), G. Lloyd, and P. Warren (Lancashire), T. Chadwick, R. Flaherty, I. Houseman, R. Parr and M. Proud (Yorkshire), S. Brown (Durham), R. Hale (Cumbria).

MIDLANDS: M. Bailey (Staffs) Capt, G. Carr, G. Coates (Staffs), M. Baker (Lincolnshire), R. Cooper (Worcestershire), T. Deas, P. Pollard, M. Saxelby (Nottinghamshire), A. Fensome (Northants), M. Fitzpatrick (Warwickshire) wkp, A. McCartney (Bedfordshire), D. Norman (Cambridgeshire), D. Williams (Norfolk), C. Wilson (Leicestershire).

SOUTH: G. Ecclestine (Essex) Capt, M. Bicknell, G. Thorpe (Surrey), M. Hobbs (London), I. Kidd, M. Ramprakash, M. Tibbles (Middlesex), K. Leppard, D. Pettet, B. Sharp (wkp), (Essex), J. Longley (Kent), J. Wood (Berkshire).

WEST: H. Trump (Somerset) Capt, M. Bell, A. Penberthy, M. Pooley, K. Thomas (Cornwall), D. Burns, C. Cowell, J. Kerslake (wkp) (Somerset), J. Lee (Hampshire), D. Graham, C. Pritchard (Gloucestershire), A. Pugh (Devon), D. Taylor (Avon).

Some great cricket was played and Harvey Trump was delighted to lead the West to victory with two wins against the clock against the North and Midlands. They batted aggressively right down the order.

RESULTS

1 MIDLANDS
176 for 8 dec (Pollard 50, Thorpe 3 for 31)
SOUTH
168 for 6 (Ramprakash 34, Baker 3 for 47)
A close game with the South only 8 behind at the end. A good draw.

2 NORTH
208 for 3 dec (Chadwick 57, Gofton 57*)
WEST
209 for 5 (Trump 67, Taylor 44, Pugh 44*)
The middle order batsmen forced a great victory in the last over, the winning run coming at the 7th ball! There had been two no-balls.

3 SOUTH
211 for 7 dec (Langley 63, Hobbs 51)
WEST
193 for 7 (Graham 47, Pooley 54, Wood 3 for 24)
Match drawn.

4 NORTH
171 for 3 dec (Chadwick 76, Lloyd 51)
MIDLANDS
165 for 5 (Bailey 80*, Houseman 3 for 49)
A close draw with the Midlands only 6 runs short of victory.

5 SOUTH
207 for 3 dec (Ramprakash 108, Ecclestone 54)
NORTH
165 for 7 Match drawn.

6 MIDLANDS
192 for 8 dec (Cooper 66, Pollard 61)
WEST
195 for 6 (Penberthy 52, Trump 48)
A win for the West and with it the United Friendly Regional Cup.

THE PRESIDENT'S MATCH

As usual President Hubert Doggart had gathered together a fine side. It was agreed that each side should be limited to 60 overs in their first innings. Thanks largely to fine batting from Wood 69 and Longley 61, a total of 202 for 5 was reached after 60 overs. After Ramprakash had been dismissed for 45, the ESCA side got bogged down and could only score 149 for 3 in 60 overs. The President's XI started well in their second innings, but in spite of a fighting innings of 60* by Martin, collapsed unpredictably against the off-spin of Trump who captured 6 for 25 in an innings of 115.

The clouds now began to gather and there was some doubt as to the future of the match. However, the batting of Ramprakash (84) and Bailey (65*) persuaded the umpires to stay on the field and the runs were knocked off for the loss of 2 wickets.

The match salver was handed over to Harvey Trump, ESCA captain, by Mr Peter Williams, Chairman of the United Friendly Insurance Company.

Teams:

ESCA: M. Ramprakash (Middlesex), T. Chadwick (Yorkshire), H. Trump (Somerset), D. Graham (Gloucestershire), M. Bailey (Staffordshire), P. Pollard (Notts), A. Pugh (Devon), M. Proud (Yorkshire), G. Thorpe (Surrey), R. Pooley (Cornwall), K. Krikken (Lancashire) (wkp), D. Taylor (Avon) 12th man.

THE PRESIDENT'S XI: A. Lee (Chigwell), J. S. Hodgson (Wellington), J. R. Wood (Leighton Park), J. I. Longley (Tonbridge), J. R. Pritchard (Shrewsbury), N. Martin (King Edward's, Birmingham), C. G. Cowell (King's, Bruton), M. Saxelby and T. J. Deas (Nottingham H.S.), J. Kerslake (Taunton), D. W. R. Wiles (Merchant Tailors).

ESSO/LORD'S TAVERNERS PRIMARY FESTIVALS
Little and Small in at the kill

If you have never seen 'pairs cricket', you have missed a treat!

The County Ground at Derby was the scene of intense activity in July, when eight Under 11 schools teams descended on the ground as winners of their Regional competitions, which had been played at The Oval, Manchester G.S., Wymondham, Bedale, Southampton, Grantham, St. Austell, Durham, Bromsgrove, and London.

Teams were divided into two leagues of four, and the winners met in the final. Little and Small were the captains of the two teams in the final! Starting at 10 a.m. and finishing at 5 p.m. four games were played simultaneously in four series of matches. Teams started with 200 runs and lost 6 runs for every dismissal. Each pair of batsmen stayed in for three overs, and no one could bowl more than three overs.

Results:

Group One

St. Mewan's (Cornwall)	212	Gayhurst (Aylesbury)	225
Yarlet Hall (Staffs)	220	Horncliffe (Blackburn)	214
Gayhurst	193	Horncliffe	216
St. Mewan's	208	Yarlet Hall	253
St. Mewan's	203	Horncliffe	219
Gayhurst	220	Yarlet Hall	241

Group Two

St. Leonard's (Sunderl'd)	205	Portsmouth G.S.	211
Leeds G.S.	267	Town Cl Hse (Norwich)	215
Portsmouth G.S.	259	Leeds G.S.	233
St. Leonard's	204	Town Close House	232
St. Leonard's	234	Leeds G.S.	279
Portsmouth G.S.	239	Town Close House	223

Final Pool

Portsmouth G.S.	246	Yarlet Hall	272
Horncliffe	236	Leeds G.S.	211
Gayhurst	242	Town Close House	234
St. Leonard's	245	St. Mewan's	238

Final Positions

1 YARLET HALL
2 Portsmouth G.S.
3 Horncliffe
4 Leeds G.S.
5 Gayhurst
6 Town Close House
7 St. Leonard's
8 St. Mewans

At the close awards were made to all teams by Mr G. Downman, Manager, Advertising and Communications, Esso, and Derbyshire C.C.C. received ESCA's grateful thanks for their generosity in allowing the use of the County ground for this event.

West Indies.

SUMMER TOURISTS 1984

New Zealand Ladies.

THE GRAY NICOLLS TROPHY FOR THE MOST IMPROVED SCHOOLS CRICKETER OF THE YEAR IN 1983

The Trophy was set up in memory of Len Newbery who died suddenly in December 1976, and had given a lifetime of service to the game he loved.

The inaugural presentation was made by Sir Leonard Hutton and the winner for 1977 was Derek Pringle. Derek, of course, went on to play for England. In 1978 Alec Bedser presented the Trophy to Mark Brearley, who went from school to Durham University and played second eleven cricket with Yorkshire. He was highly regarded and looked upon as a possible future Yorkshire captain, but Mark opted for an academic career and has been working abroad for some years furthering his chosen career.

Gordon Lord of Warwickshire was the 1979 winner, Ted Dexter making the presentation. Gordon toured Australia with the England Under 19 team and captained Durham University. In 1983 he made his debut in the County first eleven and held his place in the team for the remainder of the season without any difficulty, winning much praise from the media. A left-handed batsman and slow left-arm spin bowler, he has a wonderful temperament and is a most promising cricketer. Mike Gatting presented the Trophy in 1980 to Neil Foster, who made his debut for England at Lord's against New Zealand in 1983, and toured Pakistan and New Zealand in the winter with the England team.

In 1981 Hugh Morris received the Trophy from Brian Johnston. Hugh had made record breaking scores for Blundells School, made his debut for Glamorgan first team – and aquitted himself with credit – just before his eighteenth birthday. During the 1983 season he captained the England Under 19 team in three Test matches against Australia. Glamorgan feel that their search for a home-bred captain will end when this lad finishes his University studies. Mark Gouldstone, the 1982 winner, had his Trophy presented by Keith Andrew, Director of National Coaching. Mark had already played Essex second eleven cricket but due to an em-

Keith Medlycott, Winner, Gray
Nicolls Trophy for the Most
Improved Schools Cricketer
of the Year, 1983.
The Trophy resides for one
year at Wandsworth School
where Keith was educated.
Keith received, from Freddie
Brown, former England
captain, at the presentation in
December 1983, a handsome
solid silver medallion, as well
as two bats, a pair of pads
and two pairs of batting
gloves to launch him into the
higher echelons of cricket.
Keith joined Surrey this
season, scoring a hundred on
his debut against Cambridge
University.

barrassing wealth of young batsmen, was not
taken permanently on to the Essex staff.

Freddie Brown did the honours in 1983 when
Keith Medlycott was the winner. During the
year Keith emerged as a promising slow left-
arm bowler. He played in the ESCA Regional
match for the South against the West and then
for an ESCA team against Essex second eleven
before leaving Wandsworth School to join the
MCC ground staff. The MCC authorities kindly
released Keith for the English Schools matches
and he responded with 4 for 59 v HMC Schools
at Eastbourne; 6 for 52 in the first innings
against Wales and Australian Young Cricketers
and ended the English Schools series with a
match-winning 10 for 102 against the Scottish
C.U.Colts. Keith was capped for England
Young Cricketers in the Second 'Test' at Scarborough to complete an outstanding season. He
is also a useful middle order batsman and a fine
fielder.

The selection of the player to receive this
Trophy is entirely in the hands of the schools
themselves. They have a most comprehensive
coverage and the Trophy is open to any schools'
cricketer whose name may be put forward.
Eventually there are the schools' festivals, followed by the North of England versus South of
England and the combined schools against the
services. These cricket masters are devotees of
the game of cricket and put in countless hours of
their private time to ensure no stone is left
unturned to find the right cricketer for this much
cherished Trophy.

SOME THOUGHTS WHICH I HOPE WILL HELP YOU

BY KEITH ANDREW
Northamptonshire and England wicket-keeper, now Director of Coaching, National Cricket Association

One of the great pleasures I have had in cricket has been in managing the Under 19 Young England team both on tour and in this country. Any coach would welcome such an opportunity, and yet there is not much difference in the advice one gives, and questions one is asked, by young cricketers of all ages, at whatever level. It is particularly rewarding to see a young player suddenly 'cross a bridge' and visibly improve in front of your eyes, but this happens only infrequently. Above all else in talking cricket to youngsters, as I hope to do in these pages, it is vital to be encouraging but honest. The important thing for any player of any age is having goals which are achievable and not just 'pie in the sky' hopes. Attitudes, therefore, become the first thing to develop whatever your natural ability.

Let me highlight some of the more realistic thoughts that may be of use to players who are serious in their determination to become good cricketers. Look at your batting potential in terms of physique. Are you tall with a long reach, or are you short but quick on your feet? If you are tall then common sense will teach you to play forward strokes, whilst if you are short you will be well advised to concentrate on developing your back-foot strokes. However, having said that, there is no reason why you should not be strong playing forward or back but take first things first. Always base your game on a sound defence, without which you cannot stay at the wicket long enough to play at your best. Never underrate the importance of regularly checking basics: grip, stance and backlift. There are those who scoff at studying technique but the successful performers in all games seem continually to go back to basics if they show any signs of losing form. Practice is especially important to a batsman who can usually afford only one mistake; it is a lifeline; but again, practice must be realistic. A good coach or recommended book is your best bet to acquire knowledge for a particular skill but once you know your fault and its remedy, it is nonsense to practise without the object of putting it right; yet most players young and old do just that.

If your driving is at fault get someone to bowl or throw half-volleys to you. If your back-foot play is suspect, be sure that the bowling you practise against is deliberately short. Sometimes a negative attitude can be your problem, in which case it is not a bad idea to say to yourself as the bowler commences his run-up 'How can I score off this ball?' By doing this consistently you will forget the cramped feeling of thinking all you have to do is to keep this ball out of your stumps. Someone once said: 'If I had one tip only to give a young batsman, what would it be? I would say this: "Think of your batting as a sideways game and whether playing forward or back, look to putting your front shoulder – and head – towards the line of the ball before moving your feet."' If you do this your feet will automatically follow your head into the correct position.

From batting to bowling, a part of cricket that I personally wish I had been better at. The bowler has time to experiment because one bad delivery is not the end of the world; at the same time consistency is the key to good bowling. Another feature of bowling is that you can practise long hours without someone at the other end, unlike batting. Remember that length and direction are the watchwords of bowling, direction being just as important as length. Planning is always important and that leads to variation in pace, or subtlety. The four basics of bowling are as follows:

1 the grip
2 the run-up
3 the delivery
4 the follow-through

Here is one worthwhile tip for each:

1 hold the ball in your fingers and not in the palm of your hand
2 rhythm is the key to a good run-up, accelerating from short to longer strides
3 the delivery contains many essentials, but perhaps the most important is the sideways position at the start of the delivery looking behind a high front arm at your point of aim
4 of all the four basics the follow-through is probably the most neglected, and yet a full

Keith Andrew

and vigorous follow-through can assist all the earlier aspects of the action; finish up looking over your bowling shoulder at the batsman's wicket.

There is so much to bowling that it can be the most fascinating of all cricket's skills. Do not forget to study your field placings and try to bowl from as close to the stumps as possible, and practise, practise, practise; and PLEASE: PITCH THE BALL UP TO THE BATSMAN.

Fielding – surely there can be no reason for not enjoying fielding. Watch the first-class game and you will see that it is almost a sport in itself these days. Fitness is the key to good fielding, but determination to let nothing pass is also a very worthwhile attribute. Apart from making the spectacular catch, achieving a run-out is a great thrill and nothing lifts your team more. Good fielders:

1 are fast to the ball

2 cultivate accurate and powerful over-arm and under-arm throws; releasing the ball early is a key to surprising a batsman; very often run-outs are missed by the fielder taking too long to actually release the ball

3 do not lift their heads to watch the batsman before picking the ball up.

Remember, anyone can practise making simple catches and throws; make certain that your practise extends you all the time.

It is said that wicket-keepers are born and not made but this is not really true. The way to the top is to work at your own skill, but here are a few pointers that will help you.

1 When standing back make sure that you are well back and not in 'no man's land'. The ball should reach you normally between waist and knee height.

2 When standing up to the wicket make sure that you stay down and do not move until you have sighted the ball leaving the bowler's hand.

3 When taking the ball, adjust your weight towards the foot nearest the stumps as this will increase your speed considerably in taking off the bails.

4 As in fielding, practise hard, taking the ball from the most awkward bounces, ALWAYS using your gloves.

5 In mentioning gloves, recognise that your whole performance depends upon your gloves being well looked after; that is supple, with a good 'cup' in the palm. Nobody can keep wicket using 'boards' that have been lost in winter cricket bags!

So, I hope young readers will take some of these tips to heart. I am sure they will make you better players because you will never be cricketers unless you respect the game. Always remember that the game is greater than the player and that its traditions are worth preserving. Cricket will give you friendships for a lifetime; make sure you earn them through the respect of your fellow players.

Peter May, one of the greatest English batsmen of all time in action against the Australians. Richie Benaud waits hopefully for a slip catch.

DOs AND DON'Ts FOR A CAPTAIN

BY TREVOR BAILEY
who played in 61 Test Matches for England
and captained Essex for many years

The role of a cricket captain is similar to that of a player-manager in football, but more demanding. The main objective of both is to win matches and they must also expect to be judged by results, even if an assessment on these grounds can be most unfair. To be successful in terms of matches won, the first essential is a strong, balanced team. Provided a captain has a powerful attack, which is supported by high-quality fielding and a good batting line-up, he can hardly fail to do well, especially if his opponents are weak. Conversely, the most brilliant skipper will struggle should his side lack ability and balance.

For more than a decade the West Indies, under Clive Lloyd, have unquestionably been the world's most successful side in Tests and one-day internationals. However, few would claim that Clive is the most brilliant tactician on the international circuit, or as outstanding a captain as the late Frank Worrell.

Mike Brearley led both England and Middlesex with distinction, but he was lucky that during his reign most of the opposing elevens were seriously weakened by the loss of their most talented players to the World Series. In contrast Ian Botham took command of England for two series against the West Indies at full strength. Predictably he lost both, which would almost certainly have been the fate of any other captain who was put in charge at that time, but unfortunately for Ian it also appeared to have an adverse effect on his own form.

However, the importance of good captaincy cannot be overstressed, because it can not only make the difference between winning and losing matches, but also between players enjoying, or not enjoying, their cricket. An outstanding captain is able to motivate the members of his side and it was noticeable how well Ian Botham performed under Mike Brearley. A shrewd tactical knowledge is another big asset. Ray Illingworth's exceptional skill in this department played a considerable part in England regaining the Ashes under his command, and in Yorkshire winning the John Player League last summer, with arguably their worst ever team and a fifty year old skipper. It also helps considerably if a captain is able to contribute significantly as a player, as this allows him to lead by example from the front. Tony Greig's performances with the bat, ball and in the field throughout a tough five Test tour in India, did much to inspire his side. Two other desirable qualities in a captain are personal charm and luck in such things as winning the toss when it really matters. As there is a shortage of great leaders at Test and county level, it is hardly surprising that the brilliant schoolboy captain is a rarity.

Winning the toss sets a captain his first problem, whether to bat, or to field. Although I believe that it pays to take strike more often than not, this is not always the case and depends on many different factors like the length of the game, the state of the pitch, the weather, the composition of the two teams, whether only one new ball is provided, or the type of cricket. A captain must appreciate the many tactical differences between the normal and the limited overs game. In the former he has to worry about such things as a declaration, winkling out the opposition when they have settled for a draw, and sometimes deliberately keeping them in contention. In the latter, there are no draws and containment is more important than bowling out the opposition. Therefore he is mainly concerned with setting fields to deny runs, remembering his bowlers' quota and deciding when to employ them.

Apart from setting an example in the field, a captain is the operational centre. His players should be trained to watch him throughout the innings so that he can move them quickly, quietly and unobtrusively whenever he so desires. At the start of each over it is still advisable for him to check that everyone is in his right place. Some players are inveterate roamers and it is no good deliberately placing a fielder for a catch only to find he has moved when it arrives.

Good field placing is probably a captain's most important task. He has to be prepared to switch his fields from attack to defence according to the state of the game, as well as making minor adjustments for individual batsmen; when possible he should make sure his players know before they go out where they will nor-

Trevor Bailey batting with Jim Parks keeping wicket.

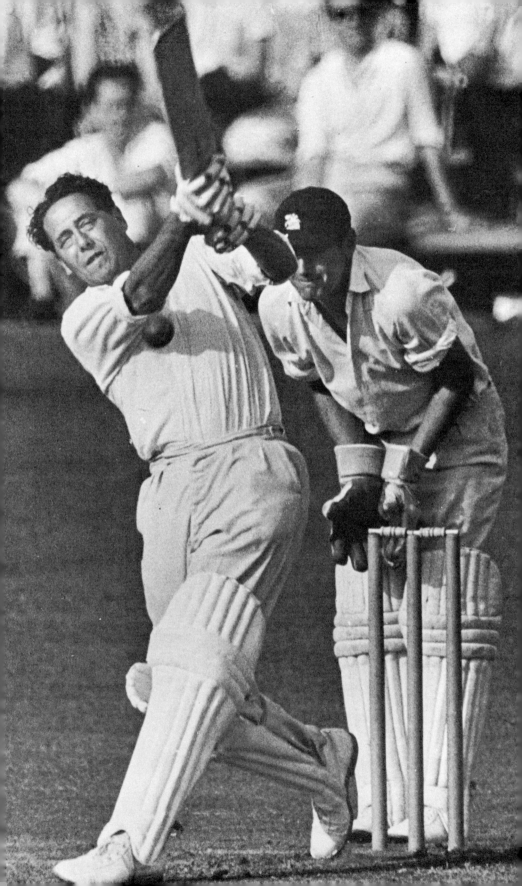

mally be fielding for each of his bowlers.

It has been said, with much truth, that bowlers win matches, and the aim of every captain is to maximise on their ability. It follows that the stronger his attack the more matches he will win, providing he handles it sensibly and sets the most effective fields which should have been largely decided before the match. Here are a few captaincy tips when in the field:

1 Avoid overbowling a young fast bowler and use him in short spells.

2 The slow spinner is often the match winner in club and school cricket, but it helps to bring him on reasonably early, before the batsmen have settled.

3 Set a fairly defensive field for a slow bowler until he has found his line, length and confidence.

4 Encourage your bowlers and do not forget to have a word with the bowler you have not yet put on, as he will already have begun to wonder why, and he could eventually be the key to the entire game.

5 Change the field for different batsmen and block certain shots, but never start chasing where the ball last went with your fieldsmen.

6 When the opposition require 20 runs to win with 7 wickets down and five overs to go, there will be great tension on the field; this is a situation in which you must, above all else, remain *calm* and *collected*; try to inspire your bowlers, watch the backing-up and make sure that the fielders in their excitement do not attempt those impossible run outs which can be so costly.

A captain also has an important role to play just before and when his team is batting. A balanced and settled batting order is desirable, with any left-handers preferably alternating with the right-handers. There will also be occasions when it pays to promote a hitter. The captain must make sure that all his side know exactly what total he is looking for, batting first, or how he proposes to reach a particular target, batting second. If he bats first and has an exceptionally powerful batting line up, but a rather insipid attack, his best chance of winning might be to bat for less than half the match. This provides the opportunity to bowl more overs, thus increasing the chances of dismissing the other side, though conversely it also gives the opposition a better chance of winning.

opposition a better chance of winning.

England cricketers are inclined to play the percentage game, which is typified by our normal approach to chasing a target. The openers usually set out fairly slowly with the object of providing a platform. Later, with plenty of wickets in hand, the tempo is greatly increased. It can work, though not always, while it could be argued that instead of asking the later batsmen to slog 6 or 7 runs an over, it would be more logical if the most accomplished players at the top of the order tried to maintain the required striking rate from the outset.

Finally, three dos and three don'ts for captains.

1 Remain cheerful and optimistic.
2 Set an example to your team by your own behaviour.
3 Never forget you are in charge. Seek advice, but remember you have to make the decisions. Captaining by committee does not work.

1 Don't lose your temper.
2 Don't show your disappointment.
3 Don't give up until the final ball has been bowled; remember the Headingley and Edgbaston Tests against Australia, when England climbed back off the floor to win.

'THEY ALSO SERVE WHO ONLY STAND...'

BY DAVID EVANS

Former Glamorgan wicket-keeper and now a Test Match umpire

'Howzat?' There isn't a wicket-keeper or bowler in the world who doesn't know the thrill of uttering that almost barbaric shout, and the crowning satisfaction of seeing the umpire's finger go up and of witnessing the batsman's dejected departure to the pavilion.

What do we know of the word 'umpire'? The word 'nompere' is the original form of the word 'umpire', a middle English word which came into use about 1362. The meaning is 'peerless, non-equal, odd man above all'. In usage the word 'nompere' developed into 'umpire', a word certainly used in sport as long ago as 1717.

There are only twenty four professional cricket umpires in the world and they officiate in the highest realms of Test and County Cricket in this country. They are employed by the Test and County Cricket Board which is based at the famous Lord's ground in London. Each umpire has to undergo a thorough medical examination before a new season begins to satisfy his employer that he is capable of 'standing' for a minimum six hours per day throughout the season. He officiates on approximately seventy days during the period late April to mid-September and in all types of weather. In the course of umpiring he may be away from home for periods up to three weeks at a time, and many miles of travel overnight may be involved before reaching the venue of his next match. He is a man with enormous responsibilities, for the laws of the game tell us that:

'Umpires are to be appointed, one for *each end* and not one for *each side*, to control the game as required by the laws with absolute impartiality...'

Firstly, it is important for those who play the game, young and old, to realise that the umpire must have first-class eyesight and hearing, with physical and mental resources to combat the long periods of 'standing' during which his concentration must never lapse. Secondly, he must be a man of absolute integrity with a judicial mind and the ability to give sound decisions under pressure; and he should perform his duties with dignity. The umpire must have an intimate knowledge of the forty two Official Laws of Cricket (1980 Code) and the practical know-how to apply this knowledge on the field. *The two umpires in a match should always work as a team with mutual confidence in each other*; they have a very vital part to play in the game and they deserve the respect and the encouragement of players and officials.

Good umpiring is of the first importance in cricket; bad umpiring can ruin a match. Boys may often have to umpire and they should regard it *not* as something to be avoided if possible or at best a rather boring necessity, but as part of their apprenticeship and service to the game. Incidentally, it can be enjoyable, as enjoyable and as entertaining as the legendary Alec Skelding used to make it for players many years ago. They were delighted when they learned that Alec was umpiring in a match, for sooner or later he would infect everyone with his humour and humanity. His booming voice greeted the bowling of the last ball of the day with the never to be forgotten expression, 'And that, gentlemen, concludes the entertainment for today!' Alec Skelding enriched life; his endearing qualities must surely have secured for him a seat in Paradise!

David Evans

Over the years the face of first-class cricket has continued to change but never more so than during the last decade. In this new era of sponsorship and One-day cricket, the players and the umpires are better paid. There are big financial rewards now awaiting the successful teams at every level of competition and with the media's comprehensive coverage bringing our summer game into millions of homes, nation and world-wide, the players' and umpires' role is highlighted as never before.

Whatever the pressures or demands of the modern game the umpire must never lose his sense of humour. To the public he is, and always will be, at best a comic character (for example when he slips, falls, is struck by the ball or collides with a player), or at worst the villain of the piece (when all stoppages and delays for rain or bad light are considered to be entirely his fault!). The reason for this humour or derision or both is a matter of deep psychology. For the simple fact is that no man can sustain with dignity the semblance of infallible judgement. Man is born to sin and error: so the umpire, seemingly adorned with the robes of virtue, wisdom, law and infallibility is a perfect target for the crowd's merriment and derision.

Time and space will not permit me to cover, in detail, the Laws and the multifarious duties of the umpires. However, I would like to discuss one or two of the more important aspects of the game that generate, possibly, the greatest interest, comment and controversy. For instance, the umpires spend up to eleven hours on the ground on most match days and even longer on One-day match days. They are the first to arrive (they have to be there two hours before the start of play) and they are among the last to leave, having ensured that all covering (i.e., of the pitch and surrounding areas) and any repair work to bowlers' footholds has been completed in accordance with the Rules and Regulations. For Test matches, the umpires appointed have to report to the Ground Authority – the Secretary of the county staging the game – not later than 4.30 pm on the day *prior* to the match as well as two hours before the start of play on each day, including Sunday. Before the start of a match they have to inspect the pitch and wickets, meet the captains and scorers to establish the boundaries and any 'special conditions' or local rules relating to that particular game or ground; see that the pavilion clock is in order, check and collect match balls, spares, bails and Match Reports from the Secretary's office. Subsequently, rolling, cutting, and marking of the pitch come under their jurisdiction, in addition to the hundred and one details that crop up in the course of play. When the match starts the umpires will be carrying the following equipment: counters (with spares or pebbles, coins, etc if used), watch, pencil and paper; MCC Lawbook, competition regulations, balls (with spares) bails (with spares); bowler's start marker (optional), piece of cloth or towelling (to dry ball), scissors/sharp knife. They may also carry elastoplast, safety pins, smelling salts etc, if space allows!

One of the most controversial issues in modern cricket is whether a batsman should 'walk' or 'not walk' for a catch behind the wicket. I have always admired the player who 'walks' when he knows that he has hit the ball. Never question an umpire's decision however much you disagree with it. Decisions have a way of evening out so that at the end of the season you can look back on just as many lucky breaks as bad decisions. In the last few years too many batsmen have adopted the attitude of refusing to walk from the crease until the umpire confirms that they are out. Never do this. The only justification for staying at the crease is when you are *genuinely* uncertain about what has happened.

Catches to the wicket-keeper, bat/pad catches, narrow run-outs and fast stumpings can be the most difficult decisions for an umpire to have to make. An umpire shouldn't put too much emphasis on a 'click' that may be heard, (sprung handle, bat against pad, bat hitting a bit of dirt or hard ground, or even, as has been known, the ball hitting the stump without removing the bail). The umpire must *see* the deviation no matter how slight. If unsighted in the matter of the catch, having made up his mind that the batsman hit the ball, the umpire should consult his colleague as to 'fact', i.e., was it a *clean* catch. Often, the batsman in completing the stroke moves across the wicket and hides the ball from view.

In all matches, but especially in the One-day competitions, where the tempo is much more hectic, the umpire in first-class cricket – with special reference to the bowler's end umpire – must move very quickly after the ball has been struck in order to get into the ideal position, level with the popping crease, to give a possible run-out or short-runs decision. The umpires, by their positioning, take care not to interfere either with the running batsman or the fielder throwing the ball. The back edge (nearest the stumps) of the popping crease marks the limit of the batsman's *safe* ground. Unless some part of his body or of his bat *in his hand* is grounded *behind* and not *on* the popping crease he can be run-out, stumped or guilty of short runs.

When the square-leg umpire's view is impeded by a fielder or the setting sun, or he wishes to ensure that there are only two fielders behind the popping crease on the leg-side when a slow bowler is bowling, he will move to the 'off side' and inform the captain and the striker accordingly. If, at the time of the bowler's delivery there are more than two fielders behind the popping crease, the square-leg umpire will call and signal 'no ball!'

Did you know that a batsman is out if a snick lodges in the wicket-keeper's pads but if a fielder uses a cap to catch the ball the batsman gets 5 runs? It is a penalty against the fielding side for illegal fielding.

What happens if the ball lodges in the batsman's pads after he has played it? The umpire will call and signal 'dead ball' (by crossing and

The signal from the umpire that all batsmen dread: 'You're out' says Arthur Jepson.

recrossing both wrists below the waist). But the ball isn't 'dead' when the wicket is broken accidentally, whether by the bowler during his delivery, or by a batsman in running.

Can a batsman score runs by crossing over before a catch is made? The answer is 'no!'. Even if he hits the ball miles into the air and runs 2 or 3 before it is caught no runs will be allowed. It is only on a run-out that runs already made are counted.

What about catches on the boundary? If a fieldsman catches a ball and with ball in hand touches or grounds any part of his body *on* or *over* the boundary line or rope the batsman will *not* be out 'caught' and six runs will be scored. However, if the boundary is marked by a fence or board the fieldsman may lean against or over the fence or board and complete the catch. Only if the fieldsman grounds any part of his body over the fence or board will the catch be disallowed and six runs scored.

Another area of the first-class game that often causes comment and controversy is the one concerning the fitness of ground, weather and light for play. In deciding whether the ground is fit the umpire shouldn't suspend play unless conditions are dangerous. The fieldsmen must be able to move about safely within twenty five to thirty yards of the pitch, with the bowlers using firm foot-holds. The ball can be dried; wet grass with a slippery ball is not in itself an adequate reason for suspension of play (although this would be a more critical consideration in the context of a one-day match). Pools of water on the pitch or ground area approximately twenty five to thirty yards around the pitch, however, would constitute a condition for stoppage. The batsmen must be able to run and play at the wicket, without restriction. Patches of wet ground outside the twenty five to thirty yard area of the pitch, or even small patches within the area can, nearly always, be disregarded. A groundsman's knowledge of the drying conditions of the ground can be of valuable help and the umpires should consider it wise to consult him. If the umpires decide, during play, that the rain has become too heavy they will suspend play. If the rain is light and the weather shows signs of clearing they may decide to continue play for a period in the hope of a general clearance. The decision to suspend play in rainy conditions is entirely in the umpires' hands. At no time, in this instance, do they consult the captain of the fielding side or the batsmen as to their wishes.

This is a 'special regulation' that applies to first-class cricket only.

When watching first-class cricket in this country youngsters should make sure that they do not get *too* dogmatic on certain points of law for at that level of the game, all the matches and the different One-day competitions are subject to 'special regulations' as well as to the Official Laws of Cricket.

Judgement on light has always brought problems, so much so that in 1979, and as an experiment, the light meter was introduced into first-class cricket in the United Kingdom. Since its introduction and continued use over the past five years, it has not only helped to improve public relations in an area where umpires could never, or almost never, satisfy the press, players, officials and spectators, however much thought or consideration was given, but even more importantly, it has enabled umpires to establish a greater level of accuracy and consistency in re-assessing light especially after stoppages. Contrary to general belief, the light meter, used wisely, is a back-up to the umpires' *own* eyesight, and *never* a substitute for it.

We'll tell them we'll look again in an hour's time just to keep them quiet.

The umpires will always consult before coming to a decision on the fitness of light. In coming to that decision they will have considered many factors. So much will depend on background, for example, trees and buildings etc, that it is possible to find considerable variance in the quality of light at each end of the pitch. The umpires will always take their light readings from the popping crease at either end with the meter held *vertically* at shoulder height, facing down the pitch. Any readings taken are noted and recorded. Some grounds are known to be notoriously bad for light conditions. Sight-screens, or the absence of them, will also affect umpires' judgement on light as well as the type of bowling. If the light is just reasonable when a slower bowler is in action, the umpires will be ready to take action if a change is made to a faster bowler, when conditions may then become dangerous. It is very important for you to remember that *only* the *batting* side has the option of continuing to play in bad light and *only* the *batting* side has the right of appeal, under the law, against bad light, even though they may previously have agreed to continue in unfit conditions. If, under these conditions an appeal is made, it will be allowed and play suspended only if the light has got worse.

When the game is suspended because of

ground, weather or light conditions the umpires will be seen continually checking outside conditions making every effort to see that play is resumed at the earliest possible moment. Following every inspection the umpires report their findings immediately to both captains and to the Ground Authority. As soon as it is decided that play is possible the players are called upon to restart the game. If the stoppage has been for light *only*, a meter reading is taken on resuming play and compared with the one taken when play was suspended. All meter readings are recorded on the Official Match Reports which the umpires send to the Test County Cricket Board on the completion of every game.

Cricket is, indeed, fathomless and we could go on indefinitely discussing its complexities, which also happen to be its glorious uncertainties. Regrettably, however, 'time' has to be called and the bails removed. Suffice to say that those happy formative years in west-Wales laid the foundation stone for a way of life which has given me years of the deepest interest and the most profound pleasure. I shall be ever grateful to those people whose interest, encouragement, loyalty and common sense contributed so much to a way of life which became an Unforgettable Marco Polo! I have many nostalgic memories of friendships made, memories which time will never erase. For me, the intangible dream of a young cricketer really did come true! Who knows, by playing, watching and learning and doing only those things which bring credit to you, your team, and above all, to the great game of cricket itself, you too one day might wish to join the ranks of those generations of good umpires who serve the game by standing.

THE STORY OF CRICKET
BEGINNING WITH THE MONKS OF THE FOURTEENTH CENTURY

No one knows exactly where and when cricket began. All we do know with certainty is that it was a very long time ago. The Bodleian Library contains a picture of a monk bowling a ball to another monk, who is about to strike it with a *cricce*; in the field are other monks. There are no wickets, but the batsman stands in front of a hole, and the art of the game was either to get the ball into the hole, or to catch it. The monks depicted in this picture are thought to have lived in the fourteenth century, and the game was almost certainly called *Club-ball* or *Cricce* or *Creag*. There is also one theory that it might have been identical with a sport played at the same period in history called *Handyn and Handoute*.

One of the earliest references to 'crickett' in this country is to be found in Russell's *History of Guildford* and a document relating to a dispute in 1598 in respect of a plot of land at Guildford. It reads as follows;

Anno 40 Eliz., 1598. John Derrick, gent, one of the Queen's Majestic coroners in the county of Surrey, aged fifty-nine, saith this land before mentioned lett to John Parvish, inn holder, deceased, that he knew it for fifty years or more. It lay waste, and was used and occupied by the inhabitants of Guildford to saw timber in, and for sawpits, and for makinge of frames of timber for the said inhabitants. When he was a scholler in the Free School of Guildford, he and several of his fellows did run and play there at crickett and other plaies.

We can assume from this that as 'crickett' was mentioned specifically it was sufficiently well known to be taken for granted.

Some years earlier than this, there was even a reference to cricket-a-wicket in a dictionary published, surprisingly, in Italy in 1595. It described the word *sgrillaire* as meaning 'to make a noise as a cricket; to play cricket-a-wicket and be merry'. Oliver Cromwell was described by Sir William Dugdale as having in his young days thrown himself 'into a dissolute and disorderly course' in becoming famous for football, cricket, cudgelling, and wrestling. This would in all probability have been about the year 1613.

It is generally accepted that the Hambledon Club was the cradle of cricket in this country. Certainly, it was the first club of such considerable strength that it could take on an All England side, but there is a reference to the St Albans Club practically a hundred years before the formation of Hambledon. An account of a great ball given for the ladies of Hertfordshire by the St Albans Club in August 1824 stated that: 'At the upper end of the room was a transparency representing the insignia of the club, first established in the year 1666.' Although in later years the game was run mainly by the aristocracy, when large sums of money were wagered, a catalogue of games published in 1720 had listed the rather more refined sports as riding on horseback, and hunting with my Lord Maiors pack; it then mentions that the more common sort divert themselves at football, wrestling, cudgels, ninepins, shovelboard, cricket, stowball, throwing at cocks and lying at alehouses: hardly pleasant company for cricket to be in! How was cricket's status improved from this degrading classification? Well, to find out we must refer back to Oliver Cromwell, for it has been suggested that in the period of the Commonwealth under Cromwell the nobility of the period withdrew to their country estates, and no doubt watched cricket being played on the village greens. When they returned to London after the Restoration what could have been more natural than to take cricket with them?

The idea of a hole in the ground instead of a wicket may sound ridiculous to the followers of the game today, but it was not until a single stump was placed at the hole merely to point out the place to the bowler that the general idea of a wicket was conceived. In 1700, two stumps were used, twenty four inches apart and twelve inches high, with long bails on top. A middle stump was added by the Hambledon Club in 1775, and the height of the stumps was raised to twenty two inches. A second bail was added in 1786. In 1814 stumps were made twenty six inches high and seven inches wide, and in 1823 were increased again to twenty seven inches. There was no further change until 1931 when the stumps became twenty eight inches high and nine inches wide (after experiments in 1929 and 1930).

The considerable increase in cricket's popularity during the first half of the eighteenth century was due largely to the great attraction it had for the gamblers. Large sums of money

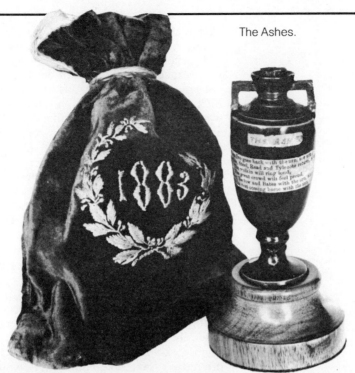

The Ashes.

were staked, and as there were no hard and fast laws, the terms of each individual match were laid down by those financially interested. The earliest known laws were framed in 1774. It was a momentous step when a Committee of Noblemen and Gentlemen of Kent met at the Star and Garter, Pall Mall on 25 February 1774 and produced 'New Articles of the Game of Cricket'. So cricket had at last achieved a worthwhile status. Admittedly, the aristocracy and gambling had been the principal factors in its elevation, but the development also owed much to Frederick Louis, Prince of Wales, who was passionately fond of the game and played it for the first time in Kensington Gardens on 8 September 1735. The Prince did a tremendous amount to help Surrey – appropriately Surrey's emblem is the Prince of Wales's feathers – and often the Surrey teams were selected by him. The Prince died suddenly in 1751; his end was hastened by an internal abscess that had long been forming in consequence of a blow he received in the side from a cricket ball while playing in Buckinghamshire. Bowling at that period was underarm. The bat, curved like a hockey stick, was designed less to defend a wicket (of two stumps only) than to carry out sweeping strokes at a ball which, because of the roughness of the pitch followed a bumpy course along the ground.

The date of the formation of the Hambledon

Club is subject to individual opinion, but it was at its height in the 1770s, and flourished until 1787 when Marylebone Cricket Club (MCC) was formed, striking a death blow at Hambledon, many of whose patrons were founders of MCC. The authority for controlling the game was shortly to pass from Hambledon to Lord's; as early as May 1788, the laws were revised by the Club at St Marylebone, and in 1791 members of the Marylebone Club were called in to adjudicate upon an umpiring decision concerning a 'bump' ball in a match in which Hambledon were playing. So ended Hambledon's authority. The establishment of MCC was linked with the name Thomas Lord, hence the name Lord's. Lord was a Yorkshireman born in Thirsk in November 1755. He was brought up in Diss in Norfolk and migrated to London on reaching manhood, finding work as a bowler and general attendant at the White Conduit Club. The club played their cricket near Islington. The Earl of Winchelsea and Charles Lennox, later the fourth Duke of Richmond, offered to Lord their guarantee if he would start a new private ground. Lord opened his first ground on what is now Dorset Square in 1787. When this lease expired the ground was moved to another site and became operative on 8 May 1811, the turf being moved from Dorset Square to St John's Wood. But in 1813 yet another move was necessary (with turf!) to the area which is now the Lord's we all know. Underarm had been the only form of bowling, but after many rows and endless discussions, round-arm bowling was legalised on 5 August 1835.

The year 1859 was a memorable one for cricket. A Mr Pickering of Montreal and a Mr Wilder of Sussex got together and made arrangements for the first-ever overseas cricket tour. On 7 September 1859 an England team under the captaincy of George Parr sailed for Quebec. The tour was a success and when news of it reached Australia a Melbourne firm of caterers, Spiers and Pond, sent a representative to England in the summer of 1861 with a request that he should collect a team to go to Australia with the idea of pioneering cricket of international standard in that country. The man concerned, a Mr Mallam, approached H. H. Stephenson of Surrey. Each player was to receive £150 and full expenses. In 1861, £150 would have bought a house – and quite a reasonable one at that – but despite this financial attraction and the opportunity of travel and

excitement, quite a number of players declined to make the long journey. When the tour opened in Melbourne on New Year's Day 1862 the crowd is said to have numbered 25,000, each paying half a crown. These early cricketing pioneers found travelling long distances in Australia a daunting task. Their second match was played over two hundred miles away from the first, and they travelled in a coach drawn by six grey horses. But the players brought home glowing reports of how they had been treated and another tour took place in the winter of 1863–64.

It was in Melbourne on a warm and sunny day in March 1877 that Charles Bannerman of Australia took guard and prepared to receive the first ball from Alfred Shaw of England in what has come to be recognised as the First Test Match. Australia won, but it was in England at Kennington Oval in 1882, when Australia won again, that on the day following the match, the *Sporting Times* produced this now famous obituary:

Thomas Lord, who founded Lord's.

First English team to visit
Australia 1861–2.

IN AFFECTIONATE REMEMBRANCE
OF
ENGLISH CRICKET
WHICH DIED AT THE OVAL, 29 AUGUST 1882,
DEEPLY LAMENTED BY A LARGE CIRCLE OF
SORROWING FRIENDS AND ACQUAINTANCES.
R.I.P.
N.B. THE BODY WILL BE CREMATED AND THE
ASHES TAKEN TO AUSTRALIA

In the following winter an England team went to Australia again, under the captaincy of the Hon Ivor Bligh, and four Test matches were played. Australia won the first, but when England won the next two, and so could not lose the series, some ladies burnt a bail, sealed the Ashes in an urn, and presented it to the England captain, who later became the Earl of Darnley. The urn was his private property until his death in 1927, but in his will he left it to MCC and it now rests in the museum at Lord's. It never leaves Lord's whether Australia or England hold the Ashes, and some of the greatest cricket matches ever played have been in what has always been known as 'The Fight for The Ashes.'

The British Army was responsible for spreading the gospel of cricket far and wide. It was the army who first played cricket in South Africa, probably after the first occupation of Natal in 1843, but it was not until the winter of 1888–89 that the first English team set foot on South

African soil. It was captained by C. Aubrey Smith, later to become a famous film star in Hollywood, and the champion of cricket in America. This tour is included in official Test Match records; some historians do not agree that it should be.

In view of the immense strength of West Indian cricket over the last thirty years or so it may come as a surprise to know that it was as recently as 1928 that England first played West Indies in a Test match. It was at Lord's and England won, as expected, by an innings and 58 runs. West Indies have avenged that defeat a good many times since, and have produced some of the greatest cricketers the world has known – George Headley, Learie Constantine, Frank Worrell, Everton Weekes, Clyde Walcott, Gary Sobers, Clive Lloyd, Viv Richards and many more.

Most of us think of the famous rugby All Blacks when mention is made of New Zealand. Rugby football is a religion in New Zealand and cricket has never reached the same plane of enthusiasm, but New Zealand have still produced some fine cricketers, though perhaps not enough of them to have produced a real threat in world cricket until recently. Official Test matches

John Goddard, Captain of West Indies, and Norman Yardley, Captain of England, toss up at Lord's in 1950 – the first time that West Indies beat England in England.

between England and New Zealand did not begin until the winter of 1929–30 when Harold Gilligan (who took over the captaincy from his brother, Arthur, who was ill) took an England side to New Zealand and played the first-ever Test in New Zealand on 10 January 1930. This was a match made famous because Maurice Allom of Surrey took 4 wickets in 5 balls including the hat-trick. Martin Donnelly, Bert Sutcliffe, John Reid and Richard Hadlee are some of the best players to come from New Zealand.

India gained Test status in 1932, yet the first recorded match in India goes right back to 1751, and India produced, long before the first Test match, one of the all-time 'greats' of cricket: Prince Ranjitsinhji, a legend in cricket history; he was followed by his nephew, Kumar Shri Duleepsinhji; both played for Sussex. In recent years India have become famous for their collection of spin-bowlers; some of them with names that twist the tongues of commentators, such as Venkataraghavan! Chandrasekhar is not quite so difficult for them, and Bedi a very welcome relief – all great bowlers though.

Pakistan was inaugurated as an Independent Sovereign State on 14 August 1947, so although young as a State it is still an ancient land and one of the cradles of civilization. It was in 1954 that Abdul Hafeez Kardar brought the first Pakistan cricket team to England, and they won a Test match at the Oval. The fast-medium bowling of Fazal Mahmood was one of the dominating aspects of the tour, but it was also an important stage in the development of Hanif Mohammad, 'The Little Wonder', who once batted for 999 minutes in scoring 337 for Pakistan v West Indies in Barbados in 1957–58. There was a long gap between Pakistan's admission to the status of Test cricket and the next country to be received into the Test fold. Sri Lanka (formerly Ceylon) played the first Test match in their history against England at Colombo in February 1982. Now they have to prove themselves in the highest class of cricket in the world.

But for all this, the oldest cricket competition in the first-class game is the County Championship in England. There will be arguments until the end of time about the precise date of its origin, but the year 1873 seems to be as good as any other, because a meeting had taken place in 1872 to formulate some rules. They were finally accepted on 9 June 1873 at a gathering in the pavilion at The Oval. The nine counties which competed against each other in 1873 were

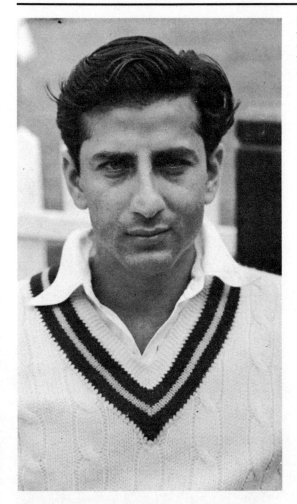

Fazal Mahmood, who took 12 wickets in the match at The Oval in 1954 when Pakistan won their first match ever against England.

Derbyshire, Gloucestershire, Kent, Lancashire, Middlesex, Nottinghamshire, Surrey, Sussex and Yorkshire. Glamorgan were the last of the seventeen first-class counties to be admitted to the Championship in 1921. One-day sponsored cricket as we know it to-day began with The Gillette Cup in 1963. That ran for eighteen years and then in 1981 the same competition became The NatWest Bank Trophy. The John Player League started in 1969 and Benson and Hedges came in to the game in 1972. Then came The Prudential World Cup and one-day test matches and now The Texaco Cup in its place.

There is so much to tell in the story of cricket that hundreds of books have been written on the subject and no doubt many more will be in the future. This short essay, however, has given a broad outline of the game's development through the centuries. There is much more to relate on another day.

THE GILLETTE CUP which was presented by Gillette to the Test and County Cricket Board at Lord's when their sponsorship ended in 1980, and there it remains.

THE STORY OF
ONE-DAY CRICKET

There is no need to say too much about the popularity of one-day cricket in England. The crowds flock to see it and millions won't leave their television sets on the day of one of the big finals at Lord's. It has been cricket's bonanza; we all know that. But how and why and when did it all start before its popularity became a landslide?

Well, it began in 1963 as an experiment. The crowds watching three-day cricket had dwindled; hence many counties were finding it difficult to keep going, so something had to be done. For years MCC had been talking about a knock-out competition, even as far back as 1943. These were the reasons given in 1943 when they turned down the idea:

1   it would be detrimental to the art and character of the game;

2   a captain would be drawn towards placing his field and using his bowler not to take wickets, but to keep runs down. If, on the other hand, he pursued aggressive tactics, he might well be assisting his opponents.

But they suggested that the talking should go on, and it did, although rarely getting past the talking stage. Believe it or not, in 1957 they decided to abandon the whole idea. This time they said that there was no practical solution for rain-ruined matches, and that there were many difficulties in fitting such a competition into the existing framework of the County Championship, and – *and we put this in capital letters* – THEY DOUBTED WHETHER A KNOCK-OUT CUP WOULD BE A FINANCIAL SUCCESS! So, to all intents and purposes, that was the end of knock-out cricket . . . or was it? No, it wasn't, because when the great slump in attendances at the three-day matches (which MCC had always believed was the basis for County cricket in this country) threatened the survival of some of the counties, any remedy had to be tried. After a good deal more talking it was decided on 20 December 1961 to inaugurate a one-day knock-out competition. The counties thought it was such a good idea – and they needed the money – that they wanted it to start

Mike Procter and Tony Brown are hoisted aloft when Gloucestershire won the Gillette Cup in 1973.

in 1962, but it was felt that the time was too short, and it was decided that it would start in 1963.

How then did it become the Gillette Cup? The great fear of everybody concerned was that the weather could make or mar the competition in its first year. If many of the matches were rained off and players had to hang about for two or three days to get a one-day game finished with few people watching, then the competition could lose money instead of making it. And, of course, there was no guarantee that, even given fine weather, the crowds, who had only known three-day cricket, would come to watch. What could be done to safeguard it? The answer was backing by a commercial company. Just how Gillette got to hear about the idea is a long story, but they did, and it is interesting that when their Chairman, Henry Garnett, wrote to Lord's agreeing to support it, he did not use the word sponsorship. He said that Gillette would underwrite the competition against loss and provide a block grant of £6,500. That same competition, now sponsored by NatWest Bank, costs the Bank over £300,000 a year. Do you want any more proof of the popularity of one-day cricket?

The Gillette offer was accepted and one-day Cup cricket got underway at Old Trafford, Manchester, on 30 April 1963 with an eliminating match. Sixteen teams were needed to make an even number but there are seventeen first-class counties, so the two bottom teams in the 1962 County Championship had to play each other for the right of entering the Gillette Cup competition. Lancashire beat Leicestershire. But the first one-day match was a two-day match – because it rained buckets, making the start impossible on the first day until three o'clock; furthermore, in this first season, it was not called 'The Gillette Cup'. Its official title was 'The First-Class Counties Knock-out Competition for The Gillette Cup.' With a mouthful like that it was not surprising that the Press called it 'The KO Cup', which didn't please Gillette too much, and for the second year it was re-titled 'The Gillette Cup'; even then a number of papers were reluctant to mention the name of the sponsor, and in some cases it took years before they did.

Another interesting point about that first season is that visiting teams did not stay in hotels. They stayed instead at the homes of the committee members of the home county. This was done, of course, to save money, but it only lasted one season because cricket is a team game and the team should be together, and also because the committee members were so delighted at having a first-class cricketer staying with them that they wanted to keep him up late talking cricket. It was only natural, but if the player had already had a long day in the field, and then a long drive, he was more interested in getting to bed. The conditions for this first match could not have been much worse and yet the newspapers could see a future for one-day cup cricket. J. L. Manning, writing in the *Daily Mail* at the end of the first day, said:

It is not possible to judge this new knock-out competition by half a match between the two bottom counties on a bitingly cold day, which is all we have had so far. But I have great faith in it. It will show what cricketers can do when they try and the standard of skill and entertainment which will be displayed in later rounds will be a much needed spur for the County Championship matches. Fears of crazy bear-and-skittles games can be dispelled. It was not festival cricket. So I am very impressed with the prospects.

Pat Marshall, writing in the *Daily Express*, commented: 'If this is KO cricket then I am with it all the way.'

Now let's switch from a rather rainy Old Trafford to the first-ever Cup Final at Lord's, and staying with the Press, here is what Peter Wilson, Fleet Street's leading columnist at the time, wrote in the *Daily Mirror*:

If there has ever been a triumphant sporting experiment, the knock-out cricket competition for the Gillette Trophy was that experiment. A year ago, anyone suggesting that, on a cold damp September Saturday afternoon, Lord's, the temple of tradition, could be transformed into a reasonable replica of Wembley on ITS Cup final day, would have been sent post-haste to the nearest psychiatrist's couch. Yet that's what happened – a sellout with rosettes, singing, cheers, jeers and counter cheers. Plus a hark-a-way on a Worcestershire hunting horn when England and Sussex Captain, Ted Dexter, was dismissed by a fine diving slip-catch by Broadbent. This may not have been cricket to the purists, but by golly it was just the stuff the doctor ordered. And I am sure Dr W. G. Grace would have been one of the doctors concurring. It's sufficient to say that the Gillette Cup may well in future assume the status of such established 'Cups' as even the FA, the Rugby League, or stretching the imagination, the Davis or the Canada Cup. And if I may slightly amend the sponsor's well-known slogan: 'Good Evenings end with Gillette'.

And how right Peter Wilson was. If you have

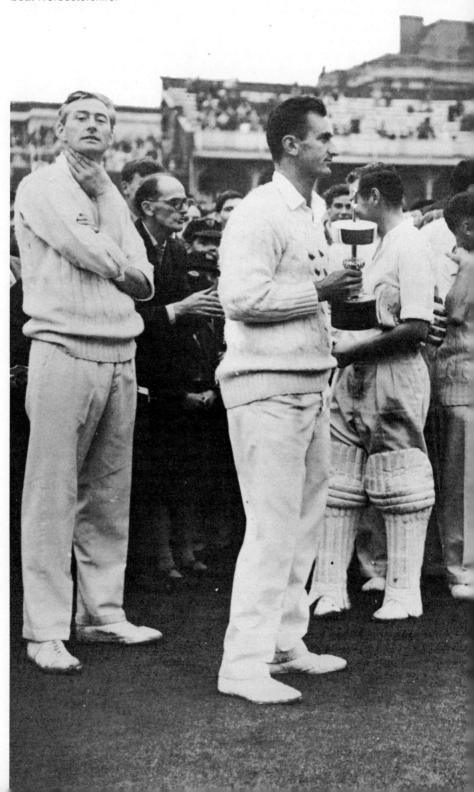

Ted Dexter holds the Gillette Cup after the first Cup Final at Lord's in 1963 when Sussex beat Worcestershire.

been lucky enough to watch, either at Lord's, or on television, a Gillette Cup Final, or now the NatWest, you will see how clever Peter Wilson was at looking into the future.

Why had one-day cricket been such a success? To begin with, there was a start and a finish to be seen on the same day. There was no such thing as a drawn game, so batsmen had to be positive and go for runs. Some of the truly great innings have been played in one-day cricket. In 1963 each innings was limited to 65 overs, but in view of the very late finishes in fading light, the number was reduced to 60 overs. Bowlers could not bowl more than 15 overs (reduced to 12 after 1963) and spectators felt that they were very much in the swing of things working out how many overs to go and how many runs were needed. It all brought a new dimension to cricket.

As an extra interest, Gillette introduced a 'Man of the Match' award. This was the origin of a Man of the Match, now used all over the world in all manner of competitions in every sport. Because of the difficulty in deciding a Man of the Match, Gillette brought in Test cricketers to do the judging. The public did not always agree with them, but the players' experience and integrity was vital. They had to decide, shall we say, whether 55 runs was more deserving than 4 wickets for 42 in the context of the result; not easy, and sometimes very tricky. But Gillette did tell their adjudicators that it could be given to a player on either side. Quite a number of players on a losing team won the award. Another added interest was the Cup draw after each round, something that football supporters had had for years, but not so cricket.

So the Gillette Cup, which ran for eighteen years before it was taken over by NatWest, totally changed the face of cricket. Some of the three-day supporters feel that it has changed it for the worse, but the hard fact remains that had not the Gillette Cup been launched, the game, as we knew it in 1963, would not have survived. Cricketers today would probably have been mainly part-time, and matches would have been played chiefly at weekends. We all agree that negative bowling and defensive field-placing took place, as it was felt by MCC in 1943 that it would, but it certainly did not hamper the development, and more to the point, the popularity of one-day cricket.

It was inevitable that its scope would widen. Some say that the John Player League soon followed. It didn't soon follow. It was not until 1969 that it was launched as a Sunday afternoon competition restricted to 40 overs and also with a restriction on the length of a bowler's run-up, which offended not only the cricket purists but bowlers up and down the country who felt that it was not fair for them to have to bowl with one action during the week and then be told how they can bowl on a Sunday. Some folk even thought that the public would not accept such a competition, but whether or not it was true cricket, it proved to be ideal family entertainment for a Sunday afternoon, for television as well as the family on the ground. Often the destination of the Trophy has been in doubt until the last afternoon of the season and television viewers have been biting their nails as they have worked out (or seen it flashed on the screen for them) how many overs there are to go and how many runs are wanted. Of course the weather plays a very considerable part, but then it has done ever since cricket was invented; cricketers know well enough that they have to take the rough with the smooth or the rain with the sun!

At Northampton the football club and the County Cricket club share the same ground, and for this NatWest Trophy Semi-Final spectators made full use of the football floodlights – a sure sign of the popularity of one-day cricket.

Now there was Gillette and John Player. Who next and when? Well, it was another cigarette company, which was not altogether surprising, because cigarette advertising is not permitted on television, so they have a good deal of money available which other producers would be spending on television. Also Benson & Hedges had been eyeing the success and mileage which John Player were enjoying through their cricket, so it seemed a natural for them to sponsor. But when they came in in 1972 Benson & Hedges were keen to be different from the other two competitions, so settled for 55 overs instead of Gillette's 60 or John Player's 40. It was also different in that it did not become a knock-out competition until the later rounds, starting with zonal tables. Certainly, their Final at Lord's now attracts similar crowds to NatWest, but the fact that the early rounds are not knock-out takes some of the spice out of the gingerbread, plus not having the excitement of a cup draw after each round.

Before the Benson & Hedges competition began in England something very significant had happened in Australia. England were due to play Australia in an ordinary test match at Melbourne on the last day of December 1970, but three days of continuous rain resulted in the match being abandoned on the third day without a ball being bowled – only the third time that this has happened in Test match history, the two previous matches being at Old Trafford, Manchester. After a hurried conference it was decided to play a seventh Test instead of the six already scheduled, but in order to give the Melbourne crowd some cricket over the New Year it was agreed to play a one-day game on 5 January. So this was the first one-day international. What happened? 46,000 people turned up to watch; that was the most important thing that happened, and the way ahead looked clear for one-day international cricket.

This time, Lord's acted fast. The Australians were coming to England in the summer of 1972 and the governing bodies sought – and got – a sponsorship for three one-day internationals. The Prudential Assurance Company offered the trophy, and a sponsorship of £30,000, £4,000 of which would be prize money. So one-day internationals were duly launched and have flourished ever since.

The year 1975 saw another momentous milestone – the first-ever Prudential World Cup. After all, soccer has for years had a World Cup, so why not cricket? Like all the other one-day experiments, it was a tremendous success. Eight countries competed (South Africa were barred): England (the host country), New Zealand, India and East Africa in Group A, the top two going through to the Semi-Finals; and Australia, West Indies, Pakistan and Sri Lanka in Group B. The weather was absolutely perfect and 158,000 people watched the fifteen matches as well as millions on the world's television screens. Prudential had chipped in £100,000 and the money rolled in. What a great oak tree it had become from Gillette's little acorn of £6,500; but Gillette started it all, and their name will always be revered in cricket. West Indies were the winners, and the whole of the Caribbean was set alight with enthusiasm. Now, like soccer's World Cup, the Prudential World Cup was set for a repeat every four years; England seems to be the place to hold it, largely because of the long distances between grounds in places like India and Australia.

In 1979 it was a World Cup with a difference. The two places allocated in 1975 had this time to be played for. Sri Lanka were there once again, but this time Bermuda were with them. The winners – exactly the same as before – were West Indies. The weather was not too good but the cricket was. West Indies were all set for the

Geoff Boycott, the highest scorer in a Gillette Cup Final, with his Man of the Match medal after his 146 for Yorkshire against Surrey in 1965.

hat-trick in 1983. Few people gave India any chance against them in the Final, but how often have we said before that cricket is a funny game. It was that day India beat the hitherto all-conquering West Indians.

One-day cricket, then, has been the money spinner, the salvation of the game. Cricket came into the sixties with a very big question mark over its future. It entered the eighties full of confidence. Cricket was buoyant; Gillette and one-day cricket had applied the surgeon's knife to the ailing patient and cured him for all time.

At the end of eighteen years Gillette gave a 'Man of the Series' award. It was won by Clive Lloyd who is seen holding his replica of the Cup presented at a dinner at the Savoy Hotel in London in 1980.

THE ONE-DAY WINNERS

THE GILLETTE CUP

1963 Sussex
1964 Sussex
1965 Yorkshire
1966 Warwickshire
1967 Kent
1968 Warwickshire
1969 Yorkshire
1970 Lancashire
1971 Lancashire
1972 Lancashire
1973 Gloucestershire
1974 Kent
1975 Lancashire
1976 Northamptonshire
1977 Middlesex
1978 Sussex
1979 Somerset
1980 Middlesex

The same competition but a new sponsor
THE NATWEST BANK TROPHY

1981 Derbyshire
1982 Surrey
1983 Somerset

THE JOHN PLAYER LEAGUE

1969 Lancashire
1970 Lancashire
1971 Worcestershire
1972 Kent
1973 Kent
1974 Leicestershire
1975 Hampshire
1976 Kent
1977 Leicestershire
1978 Hampshire
1979 Somerset
1980 Warwickshire
1981 Essex
1982 Sussex
1983 Yorkshire

THE BENSON & HEDGES CUP

1972 Leicestershire
1973 Kent
1974 Surrey
1975 Leicestershire
1976 Kent
1977 Gloucestershire
1978 Kent
1979 Essex
1980 Northamptonshire
1981 Somerset
1982 Somerset
1983 Middlesex
1984 Lancashire

THE PRUDENTIAL WORLD CUP

1975 West Indies
1979 West Indies
1983 India

TOURING OVERSEAS
IT'S HARDER NOW THAN WHEN I USED TO GO

BY JIM PARKS
who played in 46 Test Matches for England and toured Australia,
New Zealand, India, Pakistan, West Indies and South Africa

Last winter, soon after his return from the Tour to New Zealand and Pakistan, I heard a radio interview with Ian Botham. This set me thinking that in some ways touring has changed dramatically over the past twenty-five years, while in other ways making a cricket tour now is very similar to what it was in the 1950s.

In his interview Ian was talking about the Pakistan part of last winter's tour, and I must confess that I can sympathise with his comment that this was a very difficult tour. Little has changed. It is not easy for our cricketers to become acclimatised to conditions on the sub-continent. The heat, the food and the water all play their parts in undermining the health and the mental condition of players.

I well remember one predicament on Mike Smith's tour to India in 1963–64, when we turned up in Bombay for the Second Test Match with ten reasonably fit men. The rest of our party were in the Breech Candy Hospital. We did manage to get Micky Stewart out of hospital to line up to meet the Governor of the State before the match started, but he was back in his sick bed by the time the first ball was bowled.

MCC actually went into that Test Match with two specialist batsmen, two wicket-keepers – Jimmy Binks of Yorkshire kept wicket in that game, and I played as a batsman – four fast-medium bowlers, who in all fairness were not a lot of use on the easy paced Indian wickets, and two spin bowlers. The record books show that the match was drawn, which was I think one of the better achievements of the 1963–64 MCC team in India.

However, don't think I am making excuses for poor performances in India and Pakistan. To be fair, the players from those countries find conditions over here quite alien to their own way of life, and find the need to adjust equally difficult.

All tours vary, but it is fair to say that the tours to the sub-continent are the most difficult for an MCC team to undertake.

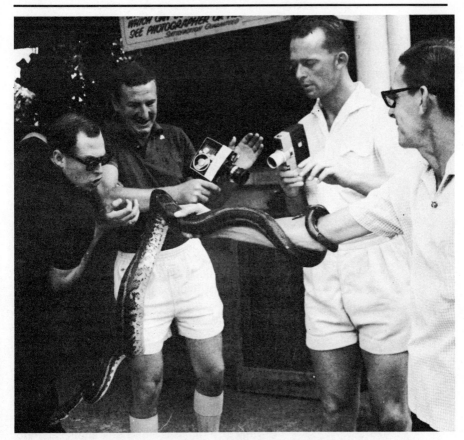

Jim Parks and the snake
at a Game Reserve,
Brisbane 1965.

Cricket is hard, played under considerable pressure from an excitable crowd, and not only are the players subjected to this heated atmosphere, but so are the umpires. And when the match is over at 4.30 or 5.00 in the afternoon there is a lot of the day left, with little to find to do in the way of using that time up. Boredom is an acute problem, and emphasises the need to pick a team of good tourists who can live together for a long period of time without driving each other to distraction.

Not a lot has changed when touring India and Pakistan, except of course in the mode of travel. My first tour there was in 1955–56, when we made the journey to Pakistan by boat. This was the ideal way to travel. In three weeks on that boat we had the chance to become a real team, getting to know each other well, and we also had the opportunity to get acclimatised to the heat and humidity that we were to encounter on tour. On that trip we also did most of our travelling by train. This was a distinct disadvantage. One journey took twenty four hours, and there was no air conditioning on the train, and very little comfort. Still, it was an experience, and did of course allow us to see far more of the country than air travel ever can.

I was fortunate in making one more boat trip with the England team, the last ever made by an MCC touring party, and this was to South Africa. The hospitality on that tour of 1956–57 could not have been bettered anywhere, and there was ample time for relaxation. And we also had time to see the country. This is one factor that has changed considerably, having time to spare. Life these days is such a mad rush, with matches crammed in, that the tourist has little chance of seeing anything of the country he is visiting. I find this a great pity, but I suppose it is a condition of modern life that is dictated by money.

Players these days get paid for practically everything that they do. Cricket is big business, and so the demands are high. The pressure is far more intense in the modern game than it ever was a decade and a half ago. Then, players were paid a lump sum for the tour, nothing more. There were no bonuses for winning a match, nothing for winning the series, no Man of the Match, no advertising to get involved with. That has certainly been a major change. Part and parcel of the prosperity that has come to the Test cricketer are the intense pressures of big business. In the past, and I talk about the tours that I was involved in from 1955 until 1968, prior to the Packer revolution, there was no one-day cricket. This type of game has helped to increase the pressure on the players. On a 'pre-one-day' tour, the team did have time to relax and enjoy their surroundings. Normally one match was played each week, and unless it was a Test match, would be of three or four days duration. If not playing, we often had the chance of a few days away, visiting some part of the country we wished to see. Of course we practised, but I do not believe that we needed to spend so much time at the nets, or trying to pull muscles in violent exercise as the modern cricketer apparently needs to do.

On a present-day tour there is little cricket other than the serious business of money-making, one-day contests or Test matches. We went on tour to play a Test series of five matches, and we also went on tour to play in as many different parts of that country as possible. We were, I like to think, cricketing ambassadors for our country in those days, and because of the way fixtures were arranged, there were always at least two matches between each Test match;

with the exception perhaps of Tests at Christmas and over the New Year. Due to the arrangement of fixtures, all members of the touring party had regular match practice, which, let's face it, is far better than any number of nets. We knew the form of all of our players, rather unlike on modern tours, when if a member of the touring party is not in the Test team, he may have to go weeks without a trip to the middle to play an innings or have a bowl. I cannot imagine anything more boring or frustrating than being one of the unlucky members of a touring party who is not in the Test team. I suppose the money now earned is some consolation for being on the sidelines. I well remember my father once saying to me that playing for England was the greatest honour an English cricketer could ever achieve, but the best way to play for England was on an overseas tour. How right he was, although I am not certain all present-day cricketers would agree.

Jim taking film before play 15 December 1965.

Cricket, and touring, gave me the opportunity to visit all the Test match playing countries on eight MCC trips. All were different, all were enjoyable, mainly because we always had a group of players who got on well together. Jet travel has changed the whole concept of touring. I suppose it has made selection of teams more flexible. The modern idea of taking only one wicket-keeper, as MCC did last winter, was not possible a few years ago. I know the argument is that another keeper can be flown out at twenty four hours' notice, but I cannot say that I agree with this philosophy. What happens when the only wicket-keeper in the party is out of form and having a bad run and there is no one to replace him? That could cost the team a Test match.

Everyone who has made tours with the England cricket team will have his favourite, governed perhaps by what success he may or may not have had, but also most probably by the climate and conditions that were enjoyed. I was fortunate enough to be involved in two trips to the West Indies. Both were experiences never to be forgotten. Naturally there was ample opportunity to enjoy the surroundings – all but Guyana are in the true fashion of the Caribbean islands, with an ideal climate and gorgeous beaches. On these tours we spent at least two weeks at each venue, and had an ideal chance to get to know the islands. The cricket was hard, every game being played like a Test match, but players were mentally and physically right to go into a difficult contest.

The leisure on board ship

Australia, playing against the old enemy, was I suppose the supreme tour, simply because we were to play against that team in those baggy green caps. I wonder if England players still get that same thrill. So much cricket is played these days, and of course the baggy cap has been replaced by the crash helmet in most cases. Touring New Zealand used to be a case of a month tacked onto the end of the Australian trip, and a chance to really relax and see the country. How matters have changed, as witness the tour to New Zealand last winter when the England team suffered a humiliating defeat; and I understand that the players had very little chance to see the magnificent countryside.

I rather feel that the days when life moved at a gentle pace on an MCC tour have gone for ever. Money has changed all that. Sponsorship, and the need to get every penny out of the public, mean that cricket must be played as often and as regularly as possible. The sponsors, the selectors, the public all demand success. To gain that success means more and more cricket, and when not playing, more and more practice. I wonder if the formula is correct. Perhaps the modern pace of life warrants the present concentrated programme of a touring cricket team. But I am certain of one thing: it would be very difficult for a player today to enjoy his tour as much as we did twenty years ago.

STRANGE HAPPENINGS ON THE CRICKET FIELD

Two Surrey players brought about major changes in the laws. The first, Edward Stevens, was universally known as 'Lumpy'. Some say he was called 'Lumpy' because he once ate a whole apple pie. Others think it arose because of some unusual part of his bowling action. But 'Lumpy' wrote his name down in the pages of cricket history in May 1775 during a single-wicket match between Five of Hambledon and Five of England on the Artillery Ground. John Small Senior went in as last man to get fourteen runs to win – and got them. But poor Lumpy bemoaned his luck because three times he bowled the ball through Small's wicket which had only two stumps. He protested, and as a result of his protest a third stump was added.

The other Surrey player was Thomas White. He once appeared at Hambledon (Hambledon of all places!) and reached the wicket dragging behind him a bat as wide as the stumps. There was an uproar and a knife was drawn by one of the fielding side, not to attack White with, but to shave the bat down to a reasonable size. As a result of this encounter a law was passed limiting the width of a bat to four and a quarter inches.

In the very early days of cricket all the bowling was under-arm. Round-arm was finally adopted in 1835 and it was a certain John Willes who played a leading role in its adoption. He apparently got the idea of round-arm bowling when his sister, Christine, bowled to him in a barn at Fonford, near Canterbury, and could not bowl under-arm because of the width of her skirt.

Can you imagine an injured cricketer strapped to the roof of a stage coach? Well it happened. In a North v South match at Leicester in 1836, Alfred Mynn scored 21 not out and 125 not out, but was greatly injured by Redgate's bowling and had to leave before the end of the match.

He reached London, but so severe were his injuries that Mr Mynn had to be packed up and laid on the roof of the stage-coach. When he arrived in Kent there were doubts whether his leg or indeed his life could be saved. Happily, both were.

Another cricketer with Alfred Mynn's courage was Willie Lillywhite. Once, when playing for England against Kent at Canterbury he was so disabled that he had to be carried to the wicket to bat. Years before that a certain David Harris suffered from gout and it is recorded that: 'A great arm-chair was therefore brought into the field, and after the delivery of each ball the hero sat down in his own calm and simple grandeur and reposed. A fine tribute to his superiority, even amid the tortures of disease.' A fine tribute indeed!

The name Cazenove will mean little to anybody. But Mr A. Cazenove once did something unique in the annals of cricket. In a game between Oxford University and Oxfordshire Cazenove obtained all ten wickets in Oxfordshire's first innings. No, this is not unique, but it is unique that he took 5 wickets in a 4 ball over. How? The umpire miscounted and allowed 5 balls instead of 4. So Cazenove holds a cricket record.

How would you like to play in three Test matches for England and not once get an innings. It happened to C. F. Root who played for England in three Tests against Australia in 1926 and didn't once get a chance to bat. In the first at Trent Bridge there was only fifty minutes play in the whole match because of rain. In Root's next game at Lord's England only batted once, declaring at 475 for 3, and in his third, at Old Trafford, England again batted once only, declaring at 305 for 5 in another match affected by rain. In the two matches in which Root didn't play, England were all out once at Headingly and twice at The Oval.

The unusual sight of a father and son batting against a father and son did happen in first-class cricket. In the Derbyshire v Warwickshire match at Derby in 1922, W. G. and B. W.

Quaife batted to the bowling of W. and R. Bestwick.

If you get discouraged because you are not scoring any runs just think of G. Deyes playing for Yorkshire in 1907. Here are his scores in 14 consecutive innings: 0, 0, 0 not out; 1, 1 not out; 0, 0, 0, 0, 1 not out; 0, 0, 0, 0: 14 innings 3 runs. You will be hard-pressed to do any worse than that!

How far can a bail travel when a fast bowler has hit the stumps? The answer is a long way. When R. D. Burrows of Worcester bowled W. Huddleston of Lancashire at Old Trafford in 1911 the bail went so far that a search was started and when it was found, the distance was measured. It was sixty seven yards six inches.

When you are playing cricket do you count your runs as you score them? Well, here is a case of somebody who did and went on counting for a long time! W. N. Rose playing at Cambridge for Emmanuel College against Caius in July 1881 scored 415 not out, until that time the highest individual score ever made in any class of cricket. At the end of his innings Mr Rose told the scorers that they had missed one of his runs somewhere and he had actually scored 416!

When very small boys are playing cricket they often have a long-stop whose job it is to stop the balls that the wicket-keeper misses. Once upon a time long-stop was an accepted position in cricket. The first wicket-keeper to dispense with a long-stop was H. Phillips of Sussex in a match against Gloucestershire in 1873. So good was his wicket-keeping that he did not use a long-stop in Gloucestershire's second innings.

If you are ever asked how far you think a cricket ball can travel having been hit by a batsman don't be caught out – this is one of the catch questions, and it has a silly answer – but it's still true. A cricketer named Ulyett batting in Manchester once hit a ball through the window of a passing train. It was recovered in Bradford!

Do you know the origin of the umpire's white coat? It dates back to 1861 when W. G. Armitage playing for United England against Free Foresters complained that he could not see the bowler's arm and from then on the umpire was given a white coat to make things easier.

Here is an interesting match. At Plymouth in 1867, the Ugly Men played the Handsome Men. The result was a draw. Perhaps it was just as well!

Here is one of the most extraordinary entries ever made in a cricket score-book.

Abdul Aziz, Retired Hurt 0. Did Not Bat, Dead 0

Playing in Karachi in 1959 Abdul Aziz was struck over the heart in the first innings by an off-spinner (not a fast bowler) and died on the way to hospital after falling to the ground unconscious. It was later established, however, that Aziz had suffered from heart trouble.

Don't be depressed if things are not going right for your team. It is amazing how things can change in a cricket match. In 1922 Hampshire were all out in their first innings against Warwickshire at Edgbaston for 15. The unkind proceeded to laugh at them, but Hampshire had the last laugh – they scored 521 in their second innings, when following-on, and won the match by 155 runs.

A match between the Gentlemen of Ireland and the Gentlemen of Philadelphia in Philadelphia in October 1892 was abandoned because it was too cold. There is a record somewhere of a match at The Oval being delayed for a time because it was too hot. Another match was once held up because sparrows kept flitting across the pitch. Pigeons have also held up first-class cricket, and in recent times, bomb scares have added to cricket's troubles, but these things don't worry anyone. The game goes on as it always will!

THE CURIOSITIES AT LORD'S

BY STEPHEN GREEN (the curator)

If you read page 973 of the 1965 edition of *Wisden Cricketers' Almanack* you will find that the then Secretary of MCC, Mr S. C. Griffith, paid tribute on the death of a famous cricketing character with these words: 'he was a ... great personality and loved publicity'. Do I hear you ask who this was? Was he a famous performer in Test matches or perhaps a stalwart of the County Championship? Neither answer is correct: the show-off to whom Mr Griffith was referring was Peter, the Lord's cat, whose ninth life came to an end on Bonfire Night in 1964! His sleek black form was familiar to many a spectator and television watcher and he served as a reminder that Lord's is not only the most famous cricket ground in the world but is also a very human place and contains many curiosities.

Did you know, for instance, that the scorer of an unusual century once umpired at Lord's? He was Mr J. Filliston, and he stood with Harry Sharp, the former Middlesex player, in the Lord's Taverners v Old England match at cricket's headquarters in 1962. His unusual century consisted in the fact that he was one hundred years old at the time! He was a very sprightly old gentleman and a pillar of the Association of Cricket Umpires.

Not surprisingly many of the curiosities of Lord's are housed in the Cricket Memorial Gallery. This international cricket museum houses, for example, a bat which belonged in 1917 to Sergeant K. Piggott of the Royal Army Medical Corps. In the First World War it was damaged in what was described as 'an unpleasant experience of bomb-dropping' and to this day it has two nasty jagged holes in it. Another memento of cricket being played in time of war is to be found at Lord's; this is a ball which was beautifully made from the string used to tie up Red Cross parcels sent to a P.O.W. camp in Germany.

Among other unusual cricket balls to be displayed at Lord's is a wicker one which was ingeniously designed in order to enable the blind in South Australia to have a game. It contains small bells and it therefore rattled when in flight. Another curious cricket ball housed at Lord's is coloured blue and not the usual red. It was commissioned by the famous firm of Gamages in 1897 for women's cricket. It was felt that Victorian ladies were very refined and sensitive and would not like to see a red cricket ball which might remind them of the colour of blood! A blue cricket ball was quickly manufactured but it was not a success. It was forgotten that a blue ball would be rather dangerous; it could not be easily seen against the sky or with the grass as background. So much for the well intentioned schemes of mere men. . . .

Some of the curiosities of Lord's are associated with the early days of tours between England and Australia. The first-ever team to go 'down under' from this country went out in 1861–62. It was a commercial venture and was sponsored by the catering firm of Spiers and Pond. A Mr Burnup helped to manage the tour and he was presented by Mr Pond with an emu's egg which was mounted and decorated with silver.

The first Australian side to come to Lord's was the aboriginal team which toured this country in 1868. One curio to survive from this time is in the museum at Lord's. It is a leowel or nulla-nulla. This was an aboriginal weapon which was adapted for cricket purposes. Armed with this odd-looking object the visiting players used to fend off cricket balls which were hurled at them from a short range!

The Ashes urn itself is housed at Lord's and is an unusual trophy. It represents the demise of English cricket which was supposed to have occurred following the Australian victory at Kennington Oval in 1882. The urn is very small in size (a mere four and a half inches high) and is rather insignificant in appearance. Furthermore it is not presented to the winner and it never physically changes hands.

When people refer to tennis at Lord's they do not normally mean lawn tennis. They are usually talking about the older indoor game of real or royal tennis. This has been played at Lord's since 1838 and the present court was erected in 1899. There are only a few places left in the world where real tennis is still played and Lord's is one of them. MCC has played an important role in the history of both forms of the game. Indeed MCC on 29 May 1875 published the very first rules of the new pastime of lawn tennis, but it was not long before Wimbledon became the leading centre of the game.

The nulla-nulla, an Australian Aboriginal weapon which was adapted for cricket purposes – to fend off cricket balls hurled from short range. An Australian Aboriginal team toured this country in 1868.

A famous feature of Lord's is the weather vane of Father Time. Not many people realise that this was not in the original plans at all but was a surprise gift to MCC from the architect of the Grand Stand, Sir Herbert Baker, in 1926. It was the only part of Lord's to suffer damage in the Second World War but fortunately it was soon repaired and brought back into use.

It often surprises visitors to notice that the playing area at Lord's is not level. There is a drop from the Grand Stand to the Tavern Stand of six feet six inches, the height, as Sir Pelham Warner used to say, of a tall man wearing a top hat.

Most people imagine that the expression 'Nursery End' is derived from the fact that nowadays it is on this portion of the ground that young cricketers are trained. In actual fact there used to be a market garden on the site run by a Mr Henderson, hence the expression 'the Nursery'.

The recent recleaning of the pavilion at Lord's has enabled one to see in sharper detail some of the splendid carving on this building.

THIS SPARROW WAS KILLED AT LORD'S BY A BALL
BOWLED BY JEHANGIR KHAN (CAMBRIDGE UNIVERSITY)
TO T.N.PEARCE (M.C.C.)
— ON JULY 3RD 1936 —

There are a number of gargoyles adorning the pavilion and one suspects that they depict important figures at Lord's in 1889, the year in which work was started on the present building. One carving bears an uncanny resemblance to the famous Lord Harris!

Lord Harris was certainly responsible for the presentation of an unusual object which is now on display in the Long Room. In the early days when a bowler took three wickets in three balls he was given a real top hat; hence the expression the hat-trick. Lord Harris renewed this tradition when he gave an ornamental 'hat' to E. G. Whateley for taking three wickets in consecutive balls in the Eton v Harrow match of 1900. The Eton v Harrow match, incidentally, is the oldest fixture in the Lord's calendar; the famous poet, Lord Byron, was in the Harrow side in the original game in 1805.

Possibly the most famous curiosity at Lord's has been left until last. This is the celebrated sparrow which was killed by a ball which was bowled at Lord's by Jehangir Khan of Cambridge University on 3 July 1936. The intended recipient of the ball was T. N. Pearce of MCC. The bird was stuffed and is now a very popular exhibit with visitors to the Cricket Memorial Gallery. It is to be hoped that many readers will come and see it for themselves.

THE CRICKETING GREATS
1 DON BRADMAN

For sheer fame, Dr W. G. Grace and Don Bradman stand apart from all other cricketers – apart, indeed, from all other games-players. The villagers used to crowd to their doors when 'W. G.' and his beard drove through their little main street. Bradman, on his visits to England, could never live the life of a private citizen. He couldn't stroll from his hotel to post a letter. The crowd wouldn't let him. His life was something between an Emperor and an Ambassador.

Although we often try, it is never possible to decide who is the greatest batsman of all time. How can we decide? Yes, you can look at their records and work it out that way, but then they have played at different times, against different bowlers, on different sorts of wickets. Has it been more difficult, for instance, for Geoff Boycott to score his many runs than it was for W. G. Grace? We'll never know. But we do know that if we look at his achievements no one can get even close to Don Bradman, later to become Sir Donald Bradman.

Donald George Bradman was born on 27 August 1908 at Cootamundra in New South Wales, Australia, and spent most of his early life at Bowral, some eighty miles from Sydney; he was nicknamed 'The Bowral Boy'. Before we talk about him, let us just have a look at some of his cricketing achievements: He batted 338 times in first-class cricket; was not out 43 times; hit a highest score of 452 not out; scored 28,067 runs at an average of 95.14, and hit 117 centuries. Just think of it. Every third time he walked to the wicket, he scored a hundred! His record in Test cricket alone is even better than that. He had 80 innings and was not out ten times; he scored 6996 runs, with a highest score of 334 and an average of 99.94, hitting 29 centuries. His great virtue for the spectators was that he scored his runs quickly. Of the 334 he scored against England at Leeds in 1930, he scored 309 in a single day at the age of twenty one. He hit forty six fours, and while he was at the crease the Australian score was increased by 506. His time for reaching 300 was five hours and thirty six minutes.

What style did he have? Just what sort of a batsman was he? Well, *The Times* wrote of that innings at Leeds:

Don Bradman

Today he pulverised the English bowling not with the abandon of Macartney who like Bradman also scored 100 runs before luncheon on the same ground, but by a display of batsmanship which in ease of scoring combined with absolute security could not be surpassed. To mention the strokes from which he scored most of his runs is to go through the whole range of strokes known to a modern batsman. Once or twice he demonstrated an idea which is not generally understood, but at no time did he take anything approaching a risk, and he cannot have hit the ball in the air more than three times during the day.

He rarely hit the ball in the air; that was one of the great features of his batting; even when he was hooking it was said that he hooked downwards. His approach was studious, not cavalier. Like Geoff Boycott, he saw his job as scoring runs, in the safest way possible, and with his natural ability – exceptional natural ability – his mastery over all bowlers was such that he could score not only safely, but quickly. He gave the game a tremendous amount of thought, and would often spend an evening in his hotel room, especially if he was not out overnight, working out his plan of campaign for the next day. Many years after he retired from the game he was asked the obvious question: 'How was it you were able to go out to bat intending to make not one hundred, but two hundred – and then do it?' Don thought for some time and then he said: 'Well, I suppose, in the end, it was because I convinced myself, without being cocky, that there was no reason why any bowler should ever get me out.' And he meant it quite sincerely.

Harold Larwood, undoubtedly one of the very great England fast-bowlers, said of 'The Don':

He was cruel the way he flogged you. He seemed to have a computer-type approach. Good length stuff went to the boundary like a bullet. He used all the shots in the book, and a few that weren't. He used to lean back and cut you or move into position for a leg-shot even before the ball was delivered. Don didn't break my heart in 1930 – he just made me very, very tired. He was the most challenging batsman I ever bowled to. He was the only batsman I saw who could square-cut me from right over the stumps – WITH SAFETY!

What did 'The Don' himself think of that innings of 334? In his book *Farewell to Cricket* he wrote: 'Whilst admitting that my form was excellent, I have always maintained that it was not such a good innings as the previous one at Lord's. It was made at perhaps a slightly faster

Four more runs for Bradman. The wicket-keeper is Godfrey Evans.

rate and included a century before lunch on the first day after Jackson had been dismissed for 1, but there were blemishes in stroke-play of which I was well aware.' How many cricketers having made 334 in a Test match would admit to blemishes in their stroke-play? Dedication and application went hand in hand with his skill.

Some said that his approach to run-scoring was almost inhuman, but Don showed the world one day that he was very human after all, and subject to just the same emotions as the rest of us. It was the occasion of his last Test match in England in 1948 at the Oval. As he walked to the wicket the reception from the crowd, in volume, would have matched a goal in a Cup Final. Norman Yardley, the England captain, called for three cheers from his players in which the crowd joined. Don Bradman, on one of the very few occasions in his life when he had shown emotion in public, was affected by this display of genuine affection, and was clean-bowled second ball for nought by Eric Hollies; it could have been a googly, but whatever it was, it was not so much the turning ball that beat him, as genuine emotion. Don Bradman had gone. Test cricket was all the poorer.

Modern cricketers will tell you that Bradman would not score the runs now that he did in profusion in his day, because these days bowlers would bowl to contain him, and not try to get him out with every ball, which is what Maurice Tate said he did with every ball in that marathon innings in 1930. Bodyline – too long a story to tell here – tried to contain him; so would to-day's bowlers, but if you have all the qualities that Bradman possessed, then he would surely have been capable of working out his way of dealing with the changes. Like the Frank Sinatra hit 'I Did It My Way', there was a Don Bradman way of doing things which was quite out of the ordinary. When he was asked one day for his secret, he replied: 'Concentration – every ball I receive I treat as if it was the first ball, whether it is the first ball or whether I have already scored 200.'

The critics who said that Don Bradman didn't enjoy his cricket have missed the real point in his case. Like the poor boy who overnight finds himself rich beyond all dreams, Bradman could never accept his fortune, his rich store of runs, as a natural thing to take for granted. He always felt he had to work at it. He may have felt too, when he had made a hundred and was preparing himself to carry on to 200, that the vast crowd

The boys are lucky as Don gives them his autograph.

had come from far and wide to see him bat and
he didn't want to disappoint them. Many a
ground has begun to empty when Bradman was
out. Writers have said before, and they'll say
again: 'We'll never see his like again.' Very few
people who saw him in action will contest that
view.

RECORDS BROKEN OR EQUALLED BY DON BRADMAN

Highest Individual score in first class cricket, 452 not out (Australia).
Highest Individual score in Test Cricket, 334 out (Leeds).
First Australian Batsman to score 1,000 runs before the end of May.
First Batsman to reach 2,000 runs in 1930 season.
Highest Individual score by any Australian in English Test Cricket.
Shared with Kippax, established a new third wicket stand for Australia.
Highest aggregate for an Australian in Test series 728 runs.
Has equalled the following:– Two double centuries in successive Test Matches.
Centuries in each three successive Test Matches 131, 254, 334.
Century before luncheon in Test Match at Leeds.

THE CRICKETING GREATS
2 GARY SOBERS

As we wrote in the article on Don Bradman, it is not possible to name anyone as the greatest of all time, but it would still be very difficult to argue against the title of 'the greatest all-rounder of all time' when we are talking about Gary Sobers, or to give him his full title, Sir Garfield Sobers, as he was to become.

Gary was a great left-handed batsman – we all know that. He was a fine left-handed bowler; in fact, he was really three bowlers, because he used three entirely different styles of bowling: seam, orthodox finger spin, and wrist spin. He was a brilliant field, and in a pinch could also keep wicket. His record as a West Indian Test player shows him to be the complete cricketer. He played in 93 Tests for West Indies, scoring 26 centuries, 30 fifties, a highest score of 365 not out, and an average of 57.78. He took 235 wickets and held 109 catches. To be such a brilliant all-round cricketer he must have had a lot of coaching, you might well think. Not a bit of it!

Gary was born in Barbados on 28 July 1936, the fifth child of the Sobers family. His father was a merchant seaman and tragedy struck the family in 1942, during the war, when his ship, *The Lady Drake*, was torpedoed as it was bringing supplies to Barbados. It went down with no survivors. Gary began his interest in cricket at the age of three; he had two brothers to play with and sometimes his sisters were brought in as extra fielders. Before his untimely death, their father encouraged them all the time, and when on leave, would play for hours with his cricket-loving children. Gary Sobers once wrote:

I have never had any coaching in my life so I suppose it was my instinctive enthusiasm for the game which made me absolutely determined to make a success of my cricket career. So above all else, I would say to a young cricketer, 'Practise every minute you have spare'. I think I can say that I practised what I preach, for as a boy, I have thrown a tennis ball about for as long as eight hours a day. Don't ever be ashamed as a boy of playing cricket with a tennis ball. I found that I knew that it would not hurt me and so had no fear. When later on I began playing with a hard ball I had conditioned myself to have no fear and I was able to apply that feeling because it came naturally when an

ordinary cricket ball was being used. I have batted
against the world's fastest bowlers after coming into
first-class cricket in 1953 and was not seriously hit
until 1961 when playing for MCC against Oxford
University at Lord's. In fact, when I first came into
cricket I used to be teased and told that when Miller
and Lindwall, the great Australian fast-bowlers,
bowled to me for the first time they would pitch short
and knock me down, so to try and give myself confidence against them I used to bat in our nets against
the fast bowlers with no pads or batting gloves or any
other form of protection. Believe me, you make
certain you don't get hit! If I had no coaching how did
I learn my cricket? How did I know what to do? The
answer is by watching great players – the three great
Barbadians, Everton Weekes, Frank Worrell and
Roy Marshall.

Gary Sobers.

The perfect example of just how hard Gary
Sobers worked on his cricket is that when he
first came into cricket he batted at number nine
and was a left-arm spinner. But his batting
developed much quicker than his bowling so he
worked entirely on his batting. When he started

to make high scores and was certain of his place in the West Indies team for a season or two he could easily have sat back and rested content with his cricketing future, but not Gary. He started work all over again on his bowling until he brought that up to world-class. It was also important that in the development of his batting and bowling he did not neglect his fielding. Every cricketer these days must be able to field.

Gary believes that one of the most important things for any cricketer is to know what he is doing wrong. Every time you get out, try and think 'why'. If you keep getting out the same way you will probably pick up the fault very easily. If not, ask other people who have been watching you. Remember, too, that you have to treat every ball on its own merits, which means that you never relax your concentration. Have a good look round when you get to the wicket and don't be in a hurry to get some quick runs unless your captain has told you to. One tip from Gary Sobers on fielding in the slips is: 'Stay down until the ball is completely played. It is easier to get up quickly than it is to get down quickly; watch the edge of the bat and not the ball and never snatch. And finally, keep fit, because cricket is a game of fast reflexes.'

So many of the more literary cricket writers have found Gary Sobers a wonderful subject for their writings. Sir Neville Cardus, arguably the most brilliant writer on the game of cricket for half a century or more, wrote of Gary: 'No batsman could sustain Sobers's immense appetite for runs if he were just a brilliant stroke-player and nothing else. No batsman can play a long innings without the power of defence. He is very strong on the back foot, which he uses as a bastion from which he forces to the off, with power and velocity, any ball which is merely a shade short in length. He has a rare store of genius.' Trevor Bailey had this to say: 'When in 1974 a recurrence of his knee-injury and the approach of cricketing middle age made him decide to retire from Test cricket, he was, even on one leg, a better and more exhilarating player than most people on two. Although he could have gone on longer if he had not experienced that knee trouble, he wisely departed from the international scene as a giant.' Sir Donald Bradman, speaking of Gary Sobers's 254 for the Rest of the World against Australia at Melbourne in 1971, said: 'I believe Gary Sobers's innings was probably the best ever seen in Australia. The people who saw Sobers have enjoyed one of the historic events of cricket.

They were privileged to have such an experience.'

And what can be said about that innings or his Test innings of 365 not out? Well, his 254 for the Rest of the World in their second innings came after he had been out for nought in the first. Players who knew him well used to say that it was a dangerous thing to get Sobers out for a duck in the first innings, because he usually came in so determined in the second innings that he made you pay for it. The Rest of the World were 248 for 6 in their second innings, and all out 514. Sobers in full cry was one of the greatest sights in cricket.

It was in a Test match that Sobers hit 365 not out against Pakistan in Kingston, Jamaica in the winter of 1957–58. At the age of twenty one, he recorded the then highest score in Test cricket, hitting 38 fours and batting for ten hours fourteen minutes (three hours three minutes less than Len Hutton, whose record he beat by one run). West Indies' score was 790 for 3 wickets, the third highest total in a Test match. One of the three wickets to fall was a run-out. The other two wickets were both taken by Fazal Mahmood: they cost him 247 runs. Worse still was Khan Mohammad who took 0 for 259. They were massacred by Sobers and Conrad Hunte who was run out for 260. This innings alone gives some idea of Sobers's tremendous concentration and dedication. It was his first three-figure score in a Test match. How many cricketers having scored their first hundred in a Test would feel they could relax their concentration and have a bit of a go with a job already well done? Not so Gary. He had the bowling at his mercy and took full advantage of it. West Indies won the match by an innings and 174 runs.

Let us look for a moment at Gary Sobers the man, Gary off the cricket field. Wherever he went he was immensely popular. It pleased him enormously that through the medium of television his cricket gave pleasure to millions. He was appreciative of the many genuine friends he had made the world over through his cricket. It was easy for Gary to win friends because he was a friend himself, and it was Trevor Bailey who put the true character of Gary Sobers in a nutshell. He said 'Gary is that rarity – a man without malice or meanness'. When the Queen conferred a knighthood on Gary Sobers in 1975 – 'Rise Sir Garfield' – and in the same year when he was the subject of 'This Is Your Life', we were seeing the measure of Gary Sobers the Man, and Gary Sobers Great Cricketer.

The third of our Cricketing Greats is the only one of the three without a knighthood, but the hundreds of thousands who got sheer joy through watching him play, would not only have given him a knighthood, but Buckingham Palace as well! It was not just the vast amount of runs that Denis scored, but the way he scored them – an attacking batsman, a real cavalier of cricket. But if those who watched him playing every attacking shot in the book – and some others that he had invented which were not in the book – thought that he tended to overlook the basic essential of defence, then they were quite wrong. Denis had been taught his cricket in the very correct school of Lord's, and it was on a sound defence that he superimposed his own technique as he developed in skill and experience.

Denis was a natural games player and would be going down in history as a double inter-national except that as a footballer his fourteen games for England were during the Second World War and so are not counted as official. But he did play for Arsenal in a Cup Final when they beat Liverpool 2–0 in 1950. His record as a Middlesex and England cricketer tells part of the story of his amazing success. In seventy eight Test matches, he batted 131 times, was not out 15 times, scored 5,807 runs with 17 centuries, 28 fifties, a highest score of 278, and an average of 50.06. He batted 819 times, was not out 87 times, scored 38,264 runs, 122 centuries, 300 fifties with an average of 52.27, and, in addition held 410 catches, all in first-class cricket. He also took 613 wickets. How does a wonderful career like that begin? Well, Denis will tell you himself:

To begin with, my father fostered my interest in cricket and football from the time I was very young indeed. He gave me all the equipment and books he could afford and unlimited encouragement and attention. If I wanted to go to The Oval to see Jack Hobbs play he would usually find a way of ensuring that I got there. I am not sure at the beginning, when I began to show that I wanted to make a career in sport, that my mother was so keen. She probably thought there were safer and more secure ways of earning a living, and it was very natural that she should; but as time went on she did approve – very much, in her quiet kind of way, and I don't suppose anyone turned up on the field with shirts and trousers better cared for than mine.

Then there were the masters at school who helped me along all they could without allowing me, I am now thankful to say, to neglect the other things I had been sent there to learn. They were pleased when I played for the Elementary Schools against the Public Schools and made a century at Lord's. And, of course, there was my elder brother, Leslie, equally keen on sport, who preceded me to Arsenal, and I am sure did a lot to make the way there a good deal easier for me. It was to Highbury I went first when I left school to go on the Arsenal ground staff. Tom Whittaker was the trainer and in the years following he looked after my training and that of the other youngsters with the same care that he gave to the great and numerous stars.

Although soccer was then my game my greater ambition had always been for cricket. Each summer I went from Highbury to Lord's, from ground staff to groundstaff. It would be difficult to find anything more effective than the training I had during those early years at Lord's. I would go into the nets and practise, playing my usual shots, in my usual style, including my leg-sweep, which even then I was using, and advice and hints and instructions would be given to me, but no attempt was ever made to change my style; the whole effort was directed towards developing and stylising the talents which I had been given, in the form in which they first appeared. THOSE ARE THE IMPORTANT WORDS. In the form 'in which they first appeared'. My batting style never varied throughout the whole of my career, though, of course, the technical execution of my shots developed and became more assured. But my method of play remained the same. For that I shall always be grateful to George Fenner and Archie Fowler who made sure that I developed my cricket along the lines natural to me.

Denis's career was not all a bed of roses because of various injuries. He was first injured playing for Arsenal against Charlton Athletic in the 1938–39 season. He had a cartilage removed but the operation was a complete success and Denis expected no more trouble from it. Then came the war and then the return to football. In the 1949–50 season Denis began to have trouble with the knee again. He played all the time with his right knee strapped. He probably played too much and put an undue strain on it. The cricket season had scarcely started when it gave way completely during the Whitsun game against Sussex at Lord's. The knee was operated on again and a piece of loose bone removed. Denis

Denis Compton acknowledges the applause at Hastings in 1955 after he had passed Tom Hayward's record of 3,518 runs made in the 1906 season. Denis also broke Jack Hobbs's record of 16 centuries in a season in 1955, scoring 18.

was out of the game until the end of July and came back against Surrey scoring a not out century. The cricketing world rejoiced. But by 1955 the knee was giving more trouble and it was then that a knee-cap was removed and the chances of ever playing cricket again were slim – unless you have the sort of determination that Denis Compton had. At first the knee wouldn't bend, so another operation was tried; this proved successful although Denis would never again have the same freedom of movement he had enjoyed before. But he came back to first-class cricket, scored centuries, and was chosen again for England in the Fifth Test against the Australians at The Oval in 1956, scoring 94. Don Bradman told Denis afterwards that it was the best innings he had seen on the tour. So it wasn't just great ability that made Denis Compton a great player: he had the courage and determination to go with it.

In addition he took the usual knocks that all batsmen do who don't flinch against fast bowling, batting once with a bloodstained bandage round his head. At his best there was no one as exciting and invigorating. His famous batting partner for Middlesex and England was Bill Edrich; they became known as 'The Terrible Twins' so much damage did they inflict on opposing bowlers. Once, at Lord's, against Somerset, Compton and Edrich added 424 for the third Middlesex wicket in four hours – yes, four hours: over a hundred an hour, Edrich not out 168, Compton not out 252 (3 sixes and 37 fours). You can score quickly if you hit 166 in boundaries. They hit one Somerset bowler for 61 in 6 overs!

Playing for MCC against Northern Transvaal in 1949 Denis hit 300 out of 399 in three hours, a hundred an hour, and it was his fourth century in five innings. This time he scored 198 runs from boundary hits. He made his first hundred in sixty six minutes, his second in seventy eight, and his third in thirty minutes. Often he walked down the wicket before the bowler released the ball. The spectators saw something that day the likes of which they had never seen before and probably will never see again. In Test matches his highest score was 278 against Pakistan at Trent Bridge in 1954. *Wisden* says of this innings:

Compton sent the bowling to all parts of the field with a torrent of strokes orthodox and improvised, crashing and delicate, against which Kardar could not set a field and the bowlers knew not where to pitch. By

Crash! – another four to Compton.

114

methods reminiscent of his former glories, Compton raced through his second hundred in eighty minutes and he made his highest score in his 100 innings for England in four hours fifty minutes before missing a leg-break from Khalid Hassan who, at sixteen, was the youngest cricketer to be chosen for a Test match.

Four out of the five Pakistan bowlers conceded more than 100 runs in England's innings of 558 for 6 declared.

If you asked Denis which Test match he remembers most he would surely reply the 1953 Fifth Test match against Australia at The Oval. He was batting with Bill Edrich when the winning hit was made and England had regained The Ashes from Australia for the first time for nineteen years. In 1983, National Westminster Bank gave a dinner to all eighteen players who had played for England in that summer of 1953 and Denis and Bill were photographed together again – thirty years on. A piece of cricketing nostalgia which brought back a lot of memories. Many could see in their mind's eye Denis Compton batting again. The pleasures he gave to cricket-watchers throughout the world will never be forgotten. There will only ever be one Denis Compton.

WAS THIS THE GREATEST ONE-DAY FINISH EVER?
DAVID HUGHES HITS 4-6-2-2-4-6 OFF ONE OVER IN SEMI-DARKNESS

Gillette Cup Semi-Final, Lancashire v Gloucestershire at Old Trafford, Manchester, July 1971

For years after this match was played, if the BBC were televising cricket and it was rained off, you could be almost sure what they would show in its place – highlights of this amazing Gillette Cup match.

Nothing out of the ordinary had happened for most of the day. Gloucestershire scored 229 and when Lancashire were 105 for 2 it looked a comparatively easy finish for Lancashire. An hour's play was lost at lunchtime because of rain and on a dull day the light was getting worse and worse. At almost a quarter to nine with the lights on in the pavilion and beaming out from Old Trafford railway station, Lancashire had lost 7 wickets and needed 27 runs from 6 overs. David Hughes and Jack Bond were having the greatest difficulty in seeing the ball so it looked very nearly a hopeless position. Any team in the world would have been justified in coming off for bad light, but with 23,520 people having paid to come in, Jack Bond, Lancashire's captain, said afterwards that no way would he deprive them of a finish; after all, in a one-day game they pay to come and see a conclusion, so he took the brave decision to bat on whatever happened to the light.

Jack walked down the wicket when there were five overs left and said to David: 'With two overs each to be bowled by the quickies and just this one by off-spinner John Mortimore, you'll have to try and hit John.' David replied: 'If I can see them skipper, I think I can hit them.' 'Have a try then', said Jack. Let David Hughes himself tell the rest of the story:

I cursed the fact of having no sightscreens. These had been taken down to allow more people to get in. The first ball was a good length. I made a couple of yards to it to make it into a half-volley and hit it over extra-cover for 4. 'Morty' then pulled someone from the leg-side to deep mid-off. I hit the second over long-on for 6, and then again through extra-cover for 2. John then bowled more middle and leg and I got under-

THIS IS THE HAPPY ENDING TO THE STORY
Jack Bond receiving The Gillette Cup at the Final from the President of MCC at Lord's. David Hughes had certainly got Lancashire there and it was Jack Bond's fantastic catch in the Final that beat Kent, and Lancashire took the Cup for the second time. A year later they were to make it three times in a row and were presented with an identical replica of the Cup by Gillette to keep for all time. How nearly all this didn't happen!

neath it a bit and found the gap at mid-wicket for another 2. Having had success with the first ball dancing down the wicket, I had decided to do it to each ball. The fifth ball was on the off-stump and I played what I think was the best shot of the over through the covers for 4. I shall never forget the crowd noise and it seemed as though thousands of small boys kept charging on after every ball and I kept shouting to them to get back. The last ball I played the same shot as the second, but remember feeling after I had made contact that it felt good . . . and it went for 6 . . . only one run left to win from 4 overs. As Jack smashed the winning run the pitch was invaded. I raced off as fast as I could. I think my most vivid recollection of the whole fantastic day was when I entered our dressing room, and the reaction of the lads. They were jumping up and down all except 'Woody' who was so overcome that he had his head buried in his hands. Jack Simmons told me that after I had hit three balls of the over he shouted out to me to calm down and look for singles. I'm glad I didn't hear him above the deafening noise.

Jack Bond said: 'The match was played under a barrage of noise and the flight of the ball was always difficult to follow even in daylight. You almost had to stand toe to toe when talking to each other. It took me days before I got over it and it was difficult trying to concentrate on other games. Never, never, never can I forget this one.'

Perhaps one day the BBC will show it again.

David Hughes pours out 24 glasses of champagne, one for each run he scored from that momentous over. He gave the first glass to John Mortimore, the unfortunate Gloucestershire bowler, off whom he scored these runs.

GILLETTE CUP
SEMI-FINAL

GLOUCESTERSHIRE

R. B. Nicholls	b Simmons	53
D. M. Green	run out	21
R. D. Knight	c Simmons b Lever	31
M. J. Procter	c Engineer b Lever	65
D. R. Shepherd	lbw Simmons	6
M. Bissex	not out	29
*A. S. Brown	c Engineer b Sullivan	6
H. Jarman	not out	0
J. B. Mortimore ...		
†B. J. Meyer .... } did not bat		
J. Davey		
	Extras (2b, 14lb, 1w, 1nb)	18
Total (for 6 wkts)		229

FALL OF WICKETS

1	2	3	4	5	6
57	87	113	150	201	210

BOWLING	O	M	R	W	Wds	NB
Lever	12	3	40	1	1	—
Shuttleworth	12	3	33	0	—	1
Wood	12	3	39	0	—	—
Hughes	11	0	68	1	—	—
Simmons	12	3	25	2	—	—
Sullivan	1	0	6	1	—	—

LANCASHIRE

D. Lloyd	lbw Brown	31
B. Wood	run out	50
H. Pilling	b Brown	21
C. H. Lloyd	b Mortimore	34
J. Sullivan	b Davey	10
†F. M. Engineer	Hit wkt b Mortimore	2
*J. D. Bond	not out	16
J. Simmons	b Mortimore	25
D. Hughes	not out	26
P. Lever		
K. Shuttleworth ... } did not bat		
	Extras (1b, 13lb, 1w)	15
Total (for 7 wkts)		230

FALL OF WICKETS

1	2	3	4	5	6	7
61	105	136	156	160	163	203

BOWLING	O	M	R	W	Wds	NB
Procter	10.5	3	38	0	—	1
Davey	11	1	22	1	—	—
Knight	12	2	42	0	—	—
Mortimore	11	0	81	3	—	—
Brown	12	0	32	2	—	—

*Captain   †Wicket-keeper
Umpires: H. Bird & A. Jepson

WAS THIS THE GREATEST TEST MATCH OF ALL TIME?
1,474 RUNS WERE SCORED — AND THE RESULT WAS A TIE — 737 EACH!

Australia v West Indies at the Gabba ground, Brisbane, December 1960

The West Indian players do a war-dance for joy as Ian Meckiff is run-out.

The most remarkable Test match climax of all time was seen in frenzied excitement at the Gabba ground at Brisbane. This was the 498th Test match played, and the first to end in a tie. It was a high-scoring game, West Indies batting first and scoring 453, Australia doing even better with 505. West Indies scored 284 in their second innings, so on the last day Australia needed 233 to win in 310 minutes. A Hollywood scriptwriter could not have produced a greater

Joe Solomon became the hero when he hit the stumps to bring about a run-out and the first tie in Test cricket.

finish to any epic film story. Spectators sat down, stood up, laughed and cried in the tension, and this is how the story went. To begin with it looked as though Australia were to be hopelessly beaten: thcy were 92 for 6. Then their great all-rounders, Alan Davidson and Richie Benaud added 134 for the seventh wicket. It was now all but a racing certainty that Australia would win. However, with only 7 runs needed for victory and about as many minutes left Benaud called Davidson for a sharp single to mid-wicket. Joe Solomon hit the stumps with his throw; Davidson's hectic scramble to make his ground failed. Wally Grout took a single off Sobers. Wes Hall began what was obviously the last over (an eight ball over), with Australia needing 6 to win. Grout swung and missed the first ball; it dropped off his pad at his feet and the batsmen rushed through for a leg-bye. Benaud tried to hook the next ball and was caught at the wicket.

The next man in was Australia's fast bowler, Ian Meckiff. It is anybody's guess what he was thinking as he walked out slowly to the wicket. The West Indian players were in a huddle obviously discussing tactics and field placings. Meckiff put the firm face of the bat to the first ball.

Off the next ball the batsmen tore through for a bye. Wally Grout hit the fifth ball in the air; Wes Hall, the bowler, rushed to take the catch himself. It would have been better left to someone else; Wes dropped it so that meant one more run. The noise was like a bear garden, excitement mounting to fever pitch. Meckiff hit the sixth ball hard and high to leg, but Conrad Hunte cut it off on the boundary as the batsmen turned for the third run, which would have given Australia victory. Hunte threw in superbly, low and fast, and Grout was run-out by a good foot.

So in came Australia's number eleven, Lindsay Kline; he must have been trembling at the knees as he listened to the sound of his own heart beating. What a situation. Last man in, with Kline no great shakes as a batsman. He played the seventh ball of the over towards square-leg, and Meckiff, all ready to sprint like a greyhound whatever happened, charged down the wicket to get the winning run; amazingly, with only one stump to aim at, Joe Solomon hit the target. The first Test match in nearly five hundred had ended in a tie. It had never happened before. It may never happen again!

Wes Hall, really fast, who bowled the last decisive over.

122

THIS **WAS** THE GREATEST BOWLING FEAT OF ALL TIME!
JIM LAKER TOOK 19 WICKETS IN A TEST MATCH AGAINST AUSTRALIA

England v Australia at Old Trafford, Manchester, July 1956

Records are made to be broken, but here is a record that may never be. Jim Laker, Surrey off-spinner (probably the greatest off-spinner in cricket history) took nineteen wickets in a Test match. It will need somebody to take all twenty to rub Laker's feat out of the record books. Here are five of the records he set up in that one match:

1 most wickets in a match in any first-class game (the previous best was 17);

2 10 wickets in an innings for the first time in Test cricket (the previous best was 9);

3 10 wickets in an innings twice in one season (Laker had previously taken 10 for 88 for Surrey also against the Australians at The Oval in May);

4 39 wickets in four Test matches equalling the number by Alec Bedser as the highest number in an England v Australia series and still one to play;

5 51 wickets in five matches against the Australians to date in the season.

England began the match in great style. Peter Richardson and David Sheppard both scored centuries and put on 174 for the first wicket. England built on that to reach a total of 459. Australia began the reply just after half-past two on the second day. By the time stumps were drawn they had lost eleven wickets. Colin McDonald and Jimmy Burke put on 48 for the first wicket when it seemed that Australia were going along nicely. When tea was taken at 62 for 2 there was still no suggestion of the utter collapse that was to follow. The last eight wickets went in thirty five minutes for 22 runs. Lock took his only wicket of the match with the first ball after the interval. From then on it was all Jim Laker. His spell after tea was seven wickets for eight runs in 22 balls. Following-on, the Australians were 51 for 1 in their second innings at close of play.

The weather changed completely on the Saturday when rain permitted only forty five minutes cricket. In that brief period Australia added six runs and lost Burke. Sunday was an atrocious day and Monday almost as bad. In two spells of forty five and fifteen minutes Australia moved to 84 without further loss. Conditions were terrible for cricket, a fierce wind making both batting and bowling extremely difficult. Special bails were used because the ordinary ones were continually blown off the stumps.

On the last day, play began just ten minutes late. The soaking the pitch received left it slow and easy-paced and by fighting, determined cricket Colin McDonald and Ian Craig remained together until lunch time when the score was 112 for 2 with four hours play left. Just before lunch the sun appeared and the ball began to spin and Laker was devastating once again. He sent back Craig, Ken Mackay, Keith Miller and Ron Archer in nine overs for three runs. At tea, with an hour and fifty five minutes left, England needed to capture four wickets. McDonald's magnificent 89 had shown that the bowling could be played. Tension mounted as Laker captured his eighth and ninth wickets. At twenty seven minutes past five a great roar went up at Old Trafford. They probably heard it in Leeds! Laker had taken all 10 wickets and 19 in the match. Jim Laker said afterwards that the best ball he bowled in the match was the one which bowled Neil Harvey in the first innings. When Harvey came out to bat in the second innings he was on a pair, so in order to crowd him, Jim moved Colin Cowdrey into a sort of no-man's-land position, but then, trying too hard, Jim made the mistake of bowling a full-toss. Neil hit it straight into Colin's hands. The great Australian, one of their best left-handers ever, was out for a duck in both innings, and he threw his bat in the air in disgust with himself. So Laker had taken 9 for 37 and 10 for 53 – 19 wickets for 90. *The tailpiece is this*: the rain was back in the evening and not a ball was bowled in any of the first-class matches the next day. Had the rain arrived a little earlier then this greatest bowling feat of all time might never have happened.

Neil Harvey tosses his bat in the air in disgust with himself when he was out off a full-toss for a duck – his second duck of the match.

Jim Laker is presented with the two balls with which he took 19 wickets by Tommy Burrows, Lancashire Chairman on whose ground the feat took place. With them is Stuart Sturridge, captain of Surrey at the presentation made at The Oval, Jim's home ground.

ENGLAND v AUSTRALIA

AT OLD TRAFFORD, 26, 27, 28, 30, 31, JULY 1956

ENGLAND

1 P. E. Richardson	Worcs.	c Maddocks b Benaud	104	
2 Rev D. S. Sheppard	Sussex	b Archer	113	
*3 P. B. H. May	Surrey	c Archer b Benaud ....,	43	
4 M. C. Cowdrey	Kent	c Maddocks b Lindwall	80	
5 C. Washbrook	Lancs.	lbw b Johnson	6	
6 T. E. Bailey	Essex	b Johnson	20	
†7 T. G. Evans	Kent	st Maddocks b Johnson	47	
8 G. A. R. Lock	Surrey	not out	25	
9 J. C. Laker	Surrey	run out	3	
10 A. S. M. Oakman	Sussex	c Archer b Johnson	10	
11 J. B. Statham	Lancs.	c Maddocks b Lindwall	0	
		Extras 2 bs, 5 lb, 1 wds,	8	
		Total	459	

FALL OF WICKETS

1	2	3	4	5	6	7	8	9	10
174	195	288	321	327	339	401	417	458	459

BOWLING	O	M	R	W	Wds	NB
Lindwall	21.3	6	63	2	—	—
Miller	21	6	41	0	—	—
Archer	22	6	73	1	—	—
Johnson	47	10	151	4	1	—
Benaud	47	17	123	2	—	—

AUSTRALIA

			First innings		Second innings	
1	C. C. McDonald	Vic.	c Lock b Laker	32	c Oakman b Laker	89
2	J. W. Burke	N.S.W.	c Cowdrey b Lock	22	c Lock b Laker	33
3	R. N. Harvey	Vic.	b Laker	0	c Cowdrey b Laker	0
4	I. D. Craig	N.S.W.	lbw b Laker	8	lbw b Laker	38
5	K. Mackay	Q'land	c Oakman b Laker	0	c Oakman b Laker	0
6	K. R. Miller	N.S.W.	c Oakman b Laker	6	b Laker	0
7	R. G. Archer	Q'land	st Evans b Laker	6	c Oakman b Laker	0
8	R. Benaud	N.S.W.	c Statham b Laker	0	b Laker	8
†9	L. V. Maddocks	Vic.	b Laker	4	lbw b Laker	2
*10	I. W. Johnson	Vic.	b Laker	0	not out	1
11	R. R. Lindwall	Q'land	not out	6	c Lock b Laker	18
			Total	84	Extras 12 bs, 4 lb,	16
					Total	205

FALL OF WICKETS

1	2	3	4	5	6	7	8	9	10
48	48	62	62	73	73	78	84	84	

1	2	3	4	5	6	7	8	9	10
28	55	114	124	130	130	181	198	203	205

BOWLING	O	M	R	W	Wds	NB	O	M	R	W	Wds	NB
Statham	6	3	6	0	—	—	16	9	15	0	—	—
Bailey	4	3	4	0	—	—	20	8	31	0	—	—
Laker	16.4	4	37	9	—	—	51.2	23	53	10	—	—
Lock	14	3	37	1	—	—	55	30	69	0	—	—
Oakman	—	—	—	—	—	—	8	3	21	0	—	—

*Captain †Wicket-keeper
Umpires: F. S. Lee & E. Davies

YOU HAVE TO BE BRAVE
TO BE AT THE TOP!

Our picture shows Colin Cowdrey going out to bat at Lord's with a broken arm in plaster, and in a good deal of pain. Colin had to go in to try and save a Test match, a match in which we saw another piece of amazing bravery by Brian Close. It was a Test match never to forget, at Lord's, against West Indies in 1963. Ken Barrington, who played for England in 82 Tests, described this one as the most exciting and tense Test in which he ever played.

Let us hear Colin's story:

Chasing 234 to win we got off to a wretched start, 31 for 3. Ken Barrington and I held firm and pulled things round. The light deteriorated, and with no sight screen at the pavilion end, Wesley Hall presented a real problem. There were a number of bouncers flying but it was a good length ball which flew, quite unaccountably, and broke my arm just above the wrist. It made the most awful noise and must have been quite unnerving for the next batsman, not to mention poor Ken Barrington at the other end. Barrington fought through with typical aplomb and then Brian Close came in to play an extraordinary innings by any standards. One moment he was letting the short ball hit him rather than risk a shot which might get him out and then, to everyone's amazement, he walked down the wicket, like George Gunn, to meet the fast bowlers. For once, Wes Hall appeared to be baffled. Suddenly he was seen to stop in the middle of his run and looked to have broken down. Worrell ran over to him and found him almost in tears, yet a few minutes later he was top pace again and the faster the bowling the more Close walked down the wicket, either to flail the bat or to be hit – and he was hit time and time again. Then, halfway through his run Hall stopped as Close walked down the wicket and he threw the ball down in humiliation and disbelief. When Brian was eventually out, all guns still firing and covered in a mass of bruises, it became clear that I may have to bat, if only for a few minutes. With the help of my colleagues I started practising as a left-hander in front of a mirror just like a schoolboy.

There were two balls to go when I reached the crease, five runs to win; David Allen had the strike. We conferred and David said: 'I have not given up hope of winning. If I have the luck to get a four off the first ball we'll scamper the last run.' Alas, Wes Hall, who had bowled nearly all day, and much of the day before, roared up and bowled two very good deliv-

Colin Cowdrey, with bat and broken arm on his way to do battle.

eries, straight, and on a good length. David did well to keep them out and save us from going two down in the series. Just before he bowled the last ball, I could hear Frank Worrell shout at the top of his voice – 'Whatever you do, don't bowl a no-ball.' 'What?' shouted Wes. Worrell repeated it twice but I don't think Wes ever did hear, the adrenalin was running so fast all round. As both teams slumped into their chairs in the dressing rooms it needed a little while and a long drink for us all to recover from it all. It would be difficult not to remember this match. Sometimes I wake up with a start in the middle of the night, my eyes open as wide as they can, peering for Wesley Hall pounding in at full speed from the pavilion end at Lord's.

Cricket will long remember the bravery of Cowdrey and Close in this match, but it did typify the courage which top-class cricketers display the world over.

Many first-class cricketers would miss a great deal of cricket if they only played when they were one hundred per cent fit. Denis Compton, for instance, had a knee-cap out after two previous operations; Clive Lloyd has had operations on both knees. Imran Khan after being out of the game for a time was fit enough to bat but not to bowl. Ian Botham has had his share of injuries, and sometimes he has not been fit enough to bowl. Tony Lock, England's great left-arm spin bowler of Surrey's Championship days in the fifties, had a knee which sometimes swelled up almost to the size of a football, but he never let Stuart Surridge, his captain, see it, in case he wouldn't let him play. Damage to fingers can be experienced, especially by the slip fielders when the very fast bowlers are in action and there are plenty of fast bowlers about these days.

Don Kenyon, Worcestershire's captain for many years, and who played for Worcester from 1946 to 1967 scoring 74 centuries, had a very long run free of any sort of injury and then – playing against Essex in the traditional Whitsun match in 1958 – he was struck on the hand by a ball from Trevor Bailey and broke a bone. The two counties met again in August, this time at Worcester. Kenyon was struck on the hand again by guess who? yes, Trevor Bailey, and what happened? Have another guess: he broke another bone!

Many batsmen, of course, bat with damaged fingers strapped up but they still have to suffer a good deal of jarring which sometimes makes them drop the bat in anguish. Helmets, of course, have provided much-needed protection against the huge increase in short-pitched bowling from very fast bowlers, but before helmets came in there were many close to the wicket fieldsmen who would stand close to the bat in highly dangerous positions. They thought it was all part of a day's work and that there was nothing special about it, but it still took a fair measure of courage. Stuart Surridge, when he was appointed to captain Surrey in the 1950s, knew he was in a side with plenty of talent – they won the Championship in all the five years he was captain – and he reckoned that he might not be able to improve his bowling and batting very much, but that he could improve his fielding, and he certainly did. Stuart used to stand near enough to a batsman to pick his pocket and never flinch; he took some remarkable catches.

So to make the first-class game you need to be well above average at batting or bowling (or both; good all-rounders are always in demand, especially in one-day cricket), or wicket-keeping (remember every team only needs one wicket-keeper at a time), and fielding. Even if you have these necessary qualifications you still need one more: courage to stand and not flinch and be able to take knocks and keep going. It's all part of the game.

CRICKET SCORING
BY BILL FRINDALL

Few scorers can claim to have been taught how to operate a cricket scoring book during a formal school lesson but that is exactly what happened to me on a rainy sports afternoon in 1949. Jack Glenister, a cricket fanatic newly recruited to teaching, had been landed with forty ten-year-olds who were extremely disappointed at being unable to enjoy their weekly games of cricket on the heathland adjoining Tadworth County Primary School in Surrey. In desperation he seized some minute scoring books from the stationery cupboard, removed their staples, distributed a set to each child and, using the blackboard, spent two hours teaching us the system's mysteries.

I doubt if the other thirty nine lads would even remember the afternoon, but I owe an enormous debt of gratitude to Mr Glenister who, almost blind and in his seventies, lives in Epsom and never misses a radio cricket commentary. I had been hooked on cricket since I was eight. My great uncle had taken me to watch my first match, a club game at Beckenham. From the moment I first stared in wonder at that sunlit scene, first heard the noise of leather on willow, and listened carefully to my uncle's commentary, I wanted to spend as much of my life as possible playing and watching cricket.

During the weekend after my unique scoring lesson I went to the local cricket club to watch an afternoon match. As I was standing near the practice nets hoping to be invited to bowl, one of the players came over to me and asked if I knew how to score. 'Oh yes' I replied. 'I was taught at school on Tuesday!'

I am sure that he did not believe me but suddenly I was elevated from a bench seat at mid-wicket to a comfortable chair in the pavilion, given a free tea and rather too much ginger beer afterwards. For the next six years, when my own playing commitments allowed, I continued scoring for Temple Bar Cricket Club. Eventually the ginger beer became shandy and then was omitted entirely!

At first I was content with the traditional scoring system. Then I read an article by one of my famous BBC predecessors, Roy Webber, in

Bill Frindall launching The Guinness Book of Cricket Facts and Feats at the Players' Theatre, London, 1983.

The MCC Book For The Young Cricketer. It featured his own variation of the Ferguson system of scoring and enabled him to record an incredible amount of detail that was invaluable to the commentators at outside broadcasts. After studying and experimenting with this system – mainly during the winter months when my father and I played out the County Championship programme using a dice and squared paper (it took ten years!) – I designed my own sheets and used them alongside the Club's traditional scorebook.

In 1954 I met 'Fergie' (W. H. 'Bill' Ferguson) at the Kingston-upon-Thames Cricket Festival. Internationally famous, Fergie (1880–1957) scored 208 Test matches, officiating for all the (then) Test-playing countries on no fewer than forty three tours. Showing me his meticulously kept sheets – he used a mapping pen with a very fine nib – he told me how, as a draftsman for the company which compiled the Sydney street directories, he had longed to escape from his office and travel the world. When his dentist, Monty Noble, was selected for Joe Darling's 1905 Australian tour of England, Fergie feigned toothache and persuaded Noble to recommend him as scorer/baggage-master. It worked, but he arrived at Crystal Palace for the Australians' opening match (against the Gentlemen of England) without any previous scoring experience – or the advantage of a formal lesson at school! He coped by copying his fellow scorer's entries throughout the match. I have seen the book in a private collection in Melbourne and it is amazingly neat. Fate decreed that the first century to be recorded by Fergie was scored by his dentist, Monty Noble.

Working in his hotel rooms during the evening, Fergie gradually invented the system of scoring which I use today. Amazingly he also devised the radial scoring chart during that initial tour. This allowed him to plot all the scoring strokes during a batsman's innings to show exactly where he had scored his runs. By adding the bowlers' initials he could show which strokes had been made off each bowler.

For the next decade my cricket scoring was limited to recording the commentaries from Australia during England's occasional tours. I played as much cricket as I could but studies and my search for a suitable career frequently interfered with that aim. After toying with architecture and publishing, I was conscripted for national service. The RAF unwittingly pre-

TIME	BOWLER (Vance Stand End)	O.	BOWLER (Adelaide Rd End)	O.	SCORING (LEFT)	BALLS	6s/4s	SCORING (RIGHT)	BALLS	6s/4s	NOTES	O.	RUNS	W.	L BAT	R BAT	EXTRAS
RCH					CONEY	34	3	M. CROWE	145	11	M 24 NB 14	71	191	4	16	57	16
41			COOK	28	P..6F	37		::.7/1	148		Round wkt.	72	192			58	
43½	FOSTER	14						3..3/4↑	154		M 25	73					
47	–·–		·–·–	29	6 6P....Y	43					M 26	74					
50	–·–	15						P5:...↑	160		M 27	75					
54	–·–		–·–	30	3.P57.2	49						76	194		18		
56½	–·–	16						3/2 2†2/3.4..	166	12	† Gd stop · gully (GOWER)	77	198			62	
00½			–·–	31	656(6)...	55					M 28 5 HR	78					
04	–·–	17				56		½/2 3/75(4) .4.4↑	171	14	helmet hit	79	207			71	
09			–·–	32				5B 845P•7 .24..	177	15	Over wkt. (SB) So p'ship · 73 min	80	219			78	21
14	–·–	18						6.:...	183		M 29	81					
17			–·–	33	P.·6...	62					Round wkt. M 30	82					
20	–·–	19						8....7 4....	189	16		83	223			82	
24			–··–	34	3.4....	68	4					84	227		22		
26	–·–	20						...3.	195		M 31	85					
30			BOTHAM	18	1:.. 43/74BE .41	73	5	G	196		† NEW BALL	86	232		27		
34	WILLIS	15			:.2 88 .4.	79	6					87	236		31		
39			–·–	19				34..8P6	202		M 32	88					
42/45	DRINKS –··–	16			5 19 .1	81		6 4/5 .4..	206	17	CROWE 27' on 82. ↑	89	241		32	86	
49			–·–	20	†8: ..†.†2 4	87	7				° Just short of COOK (op 24/168), NZ a lead	90	247		38		
53	–·–	17						:. 8.6	212			91	248			87	
58			–·–	21	6 83E ..1	90		:†	215			92	250		39	88	
01	–·–	18			7 1	91		...2	220		6 HR	93	251		40		
05			–·–	22	†8/7† 7.:3x 4	97	8				× Almost bowled.	94	255		44		
09	–·–	19						†:..2†.	226		† Gd stop · gully (GOWER) M 33	95					
13			–·–	23	78 .1	99		...3/4	230			96	256		45		
16½	–·–	20			:.†.:†9 .1	104		.:	231			97	257		46		
21			–·–	24	†12..9 44.1	108	10	3:	233		CONEY's 50: 142' 100 p'ship : 142 min	98	266		55		
25	–·–	21			4..†2†..:	114					M 34	99					
29			–·–	25				4 20 7 75 ..4.41	239	19	° Hard chance · gully (GOWER) 31' on 88	100	275			97	
32½	–··–	22			:..:	117		7L4/5 .3	242		M. CROWE's 82: 273'	101	278			100	
38			GATTING	1		117	10	:.:+W	245	19	(W)	101	279	5	55	100	22
40	TEA							HADLEE		LHB	M 34 NB 14				T	E	A
20			GATTING	1				3†3 ..2	3		† St. attempt (leg side)	102	281			2	
22½	BOTHAM	26			7 .1	118		†3.:†4	8			103	282		56		
28			–·–	2	:..: 8 .4.	124					M 35	104					
10	–·–	27			2/3·½ .4	127	11	8(4)3/4†9 441	11	2		105	295		60	11	
15			–·–	3	..:	129		7.344 2.40①	16	3	NB 15	106	302			18	
20	FOSTER	21						4.2 ..W	19	3	Botham off · Fowler sub.	106	302	6	60	18	22
21								SNEDDEN		LHB						0	
23	–·–	21			3↑ 4.	131	12	8 .1	1		7 HR	107	307		64	1	
26			COOK	35	:.. 7/8	135		8 :	3		Over wkt. to LHB	108	309		65	2	
30	–·–	22			9 3P.	139	12	4 9 .1	5	–	M 35 NB 15 Botham back.	109	311	6	66	3	22

© 1984 BILL FRINDALL

pared me admirably for my present work as a cricket statistician and scorer. I was given a grounding in draftsmanship, an insight into statistics and accountancy – even a simulation of my Test Match Special role by being sent monthly into a NATO bunker beneath Fontainebleau Forest to record hits and missiles of mock world wars (we lost fourteen–six)!

The end of my short service commission coincided with the sudden death of my predecessor on radio, Arthur Wrigley. That announcement prompted me to write to the Head of BBC Radio Outside Broadcasts offering my services. Incredibly my daring resulted in an interview which led to my joining the TMS team at Old Trafford, Manchester, on 2 June 1966. The commentary team included John Arlott, Robert Hudson, Roy Lawrence, Norman Yardley, Freddie Brown and Jim Swanton. After Brian Johnston (then with television) had slipped a Test Match Broadcasters' Club tie round my neck ('That will be £1 please!,), I was immediately in action. The very first ball of the match, bowled by Jeff Jones of Glamorgan, was savaged to the cover-point boundary by Conrad Hunte. Now, eighteen years later, I am about to score my hundredth Test match for the BBC. Little did Jack Glenister realise the effect of that scoring lesson!

My scoring system has been explained in several of my books, including all six volumes of *Frindall's Score Book* which covered various Test series between 1975 and 1980. Most recently it appeared in the first edition of *Test Match Special*, published by Queen Anne Press in 1981. Although there is not room here for me to go into much detail, I thought that you might like to see my ball-by-ball sheet and radial scoring chart of Martin Crowe's first century in Test cricket, scored against England at Wellington at the beginning of this year.

My method is to use basic conventions of the standard or traditional system of scoring as described in *Cricket Umpiring and Scoring*, a textbook for umpires and scorers compiled by R. S. Rait Kerr. I have added a number of symbols above each ball received by the batsmen to show exactly what happened to it:

B	Bye
E	Edged stroke
EP	Edged ball into pads
F	Full toss
G	Hit on glove

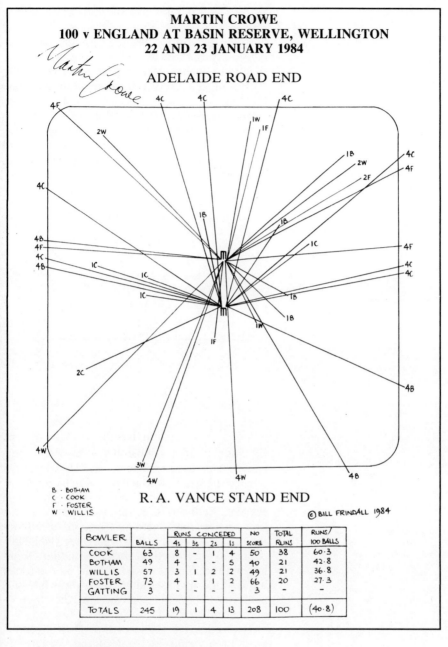

MARTIN CROWE
100 v ENGLAND AT BASIN RESERVE, WELLINGTON
22 AND 23 JANUARY 1984

ADELAIDE ROAD END

R. A. VANCE STAND END

B · BOTHAM
C · COOK
F · FOSTER
W · WILLIS

© BILL FRINDALL 1984

BOWLER	BALLS	RUNS CONCEDED				NO SCORE	TOTAL RUNS	RUNS/ 100 BALLS
		4s	3s	2s	1s			
COOK	63	8	-	1	4	50	38	60·3
BOTHAM	49	4	-	-	5	40	21	42·8
WILLIS	57	3	1	2	2	49	21	36·8
FOSTER	73	4	-	1	2	66	20	27·3
GATTING	3	-	-	-	-	3	-	-
TOTALS	245	19	1	4	13	208	100	(40·8)

L	Hit on pad – lbw appeal
LB	Leg bye
P	Hit on pad – no appeal
S	Sharp (quick) single
X	Played and missed
Y	Yorker
↑	Bouncer
↓	Shooter

A dot above the dot denoting a ball from which no runs have been scored shows that the batsman played the ball defensively. If there is no symbol or dot above the lower dot then the batsman played no stroke to the ball. By this means you can chart the accuracy of the bowling.

The numbers above dots and scoring strokes show the area of the field into which the batsman has hit the ball. It is based on the following key which is reversed for left-handed batsmen:

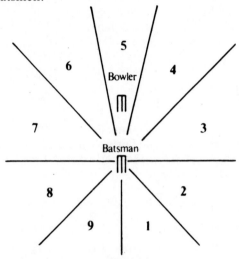

By studying my scoresheet it is possible to tell exactly what has happened to each bowler; who bowled the ball to whom, from which end of the ground, at what time, and how the batsman reacted. Reduced to its bare essentials, the system requires only one digit to record each scoring stroke. Less recording is necessary while the over is in progress than with the standard scoring method. Unless a wicket falls, all the totalling is done at the end of the over while the fielders are changing positions and when there is no action to record.

The radial chart shows that Crowe scored most of his runs in front of the wicket, his proportion of boundaries – 76 of his 100 runs came in fours – being particularly high for a Test match innings, especially when the highest score of his previous thirteen innings was only 46.

I hope that this chapter has shown how much I enjoy my work, which is really a hobby that has got out of control. And if ever your teacher decides to show you how to score, make sure that you pay attention.

GIRLS PLAYING CRICKET!
IS THIS SOMETHING NEW?

If you think that girls playing cricket is something new that has developed during the recent battle for equality of the sexes, then you must think again. Our picture shows a match between the Ladies of Rochester and the Ladies of Maidstone in 1838, and there is no reason to doubt that when boys started playing cricket in the very early days of the game's existence, their sisters often took part. There are many references to women playing cricket in the eighteenth century, and although some of the paintings suggest rather bawdy occasions, there was much less chance of injury then than there is now. There wasn't such a thing as a bumper, and the shape of the bat compelled the batsman or batswoman to stand fairly clear of the line of the ball's delivery, so that early women cricketers did not need to fear the possibility of injury.

Organised women's cricket seems to have started towards the end of the 1880s. The White Heather Cricket Club, the first known women's cricket club, came into existence in 1887. Within a few years of this, there were women's cricket clubs in Australia. NDCB stands for Nederlandse Dames Cricket Bond, the Dutch equivalent of the Women's Cricket Association.

One of the strangest stories concerning women's cricket happened in 1939, the year of the outbreak of the Second World War. Two schoolgirl elevens were selected from Harrogate College, Roedean, Cheltenham Ladies' College and Beehive, Bexhill to introduce the game to schools in Canada at the invitation of

Ladies of Rochester versus Ladies of Maidstone, July 1838.

the Overseas Education League of Canada. It is strange that there should have been a schoolboys' and a schoolgirls' tour to Canada in that last pre-war season, both stranded on the wrong side of the Atlantic when war began, and from both teams, some who stayed. There are details available in the records of the schoolboys' tour but absolutely nothing is known of the schoolgirls' tour. They sailed on 8 July and should have left Canada on 9 September (six days after war had broken out). The Canadian Cricket Association have no details and even wondered whether someone had muddled them up with the boys. There is no doubt that the tour took place. What happened? Does anyone know? There must be someone alive who went to Harrogate College, Roedean, Cheltenham Ladies' College or Beehive, Bexhill, who went on the tour.

Tours have been very much part and parcel of women's cricket. In the winter of 1934–35 England sent a team to Australia and New Zealand, playing three Tests in Australia, winning two and drawing one, and winning the only one played in New Zealand. In the first ever women's Test match in Brisbane when Australia were bowled out for 47, Miss M. Maclagen took 7 wickets for 10 runs. She was still taking wickets in Test matches in 1951 with 5 for 43 at Scarborough. She also scored a century in that second Test in Australia at Sydney.

A household name in women's cricket in recent years, of course, has been Rachael Heyhoe Flint, but it must not be thought that she alone has been responsible for the marked improvement in women's cricket, although her skill as a player and immense enthusiasm have had a great deal to do with it. Rachael's sporting talents were exceptional. She kept goal for England's hockey team, was a county squash player and captain of England women's cricket team. In fact her sacking from the England captaincy in 1977 achieved nearly as much space in the media as the Boycott affair has done in 1983. However, she did achieve two great ambitions: for women to play at Lord's, and a Women's World Cup which England won when she was captain.

So women's cricket thrives, and of course women have a tremendous interest in cricket on television. So a Young Cricketer can be of either sex, and has been a for very long time – several hundred years!

THOSE TWO OLD PALS OF MINE, RAMADHIN AND VALENTINE
A PIECE OF CRICKET MAGIC

This is a story with a difference. It isn't just the story of two bowlers doing well in a Test series. It's a little piece of cricket magic. At the beginning of the summer in 1950, England's cricketers and supporters awaited the arrival of the West Indies touring team. The West Indies had never won a Test match in England. The world knew they had some fine batsmen and their fast bowling was likely to be useful, but it was thought that their great weakness on English wickets would be their spin bowling, as they were bringing two virtual unknowns, 'Sonny' Ramadhin and Alfred Valentine. What happened? Well, these two destroyed the cream of English batting and West Indies won; not only was this their first win on English soil at Lord's, but they took the series by three matches to one. West Indian calypso writers were springing up everywhere with something to rhyme with Valentine. Here is one that tells just how West Indian people felt about them:

> With Ramadhin and Valentine
> And give me any nine
> And we can beat England any time.

Sonny Ramadhin was an orphan brought up by his grandmother. The only chance he had to play cricket as a youngster was on the streets or in some clearing among the sugar-cane fields which surrounded where he lived; sometimes a dustbin was the stumps and the bat was shaped out of the stem of a coconut leaf. But in these primitive conditions he had shown a most extraordinary gift. He could bowl a leg-spinner almost with the identical action that he used for an off-spinner, so similar in fact that batsmen could not decide which was which.

One day, Clarence Skinner, a cricketer himself, was watching some lads playing in a public park. He noticed a little fellow bowling, and from where he stood he could not decide which way the ball was turning all the time. So Skinner invited him to come and bowl at some nets. Skinner was confident that he had unearthed something very original – and he had!

'Sonny' (this was his only name; someone

gave him the initials 'K.T.' but this was fictitious) bowled his way into the Trinidad team which played in February 1950. Should they pick him to tour England? He was only twenty years of age, and so slight that they doubted his ability to stand up physically to a tour of England, and, of course, he had virtually no experience. They picked him, and Jeff Stollmeyer, captain of that successful 1950 side wrote of Ramadhin: 'Everything in those times was novel to him. He had never been on a ship before, never been out of Trinidad, the menu card on the morning breakfast table presented a difficulty; the diet was different, even the double-decker buses in London were a novelty. "Let's ride in one of those upstairs buses", he suggested to me one day. It is true that when he bowled to Len Hutton at Bradford, he didn't know Len even by reputation. Hutton was just another batsman to him.'

Why was he such a success? Well, his length and direction were immaculate to begin with, the basic ingredient, of all good bowling. Then, of course, he had deception up his sleeve – off-break or leg-break with the same action. And the deception was up his sleeve because he always bowled with his sleeves rolled down and neatly buttoned. He felt that with his sleeves down it might be more difficult for batsmen to gauge what he was going to bowl as his arm came over. He usually bowled wearing his cap. There appears to be no reason for this except perhaps that it was something different, and he was certainly a 'something different' bowler. He was a mystery bowler because he was different from all other known off-break bowlers. He did not cut the ball down with the palm of his hand facing his body, but rather the palm appeared to be thrown at the batsman. This opened up an avenue for deception with his leg-break which he mostly rolled. The quicker ball which he pushed through was just one extra hazard for the batsman when it was taking him all his time trying to spot the off-break or leg-break. Contrary to a lot of cricket talk, Ramadhin did not bowl a googly. It was a straightforward off-break or leg-break. It was said afterwards that by some particular mannerism the West Indies players in the field could always tell what was coming. In fact it was said that Frank Worrell could sometimes be seen moving in the slips in readiness for what he knew was to be bowled. But the English batsmen never did. Ramadhin bowled eleven consecutive maidens at Lord's.

'Sonny' Ramadhin: the maker of magic in action as the batsman tries to fathom out what is coming next!

Cricket history is cluttered with stories of great bowlers who hunted in pairs. Lindwall and Miller, Statham and Trueman, Lock and Laker. 'Sonny' Ramadhin certainly had a partner in crime on this tour, the other inexperienced bowler, Alfred Valentine, as different from 'Sonny' as chalk from cheese. He was left-handed, for a start, a conventional left-hander depending on spin and flight for reward. Batsmen who had become absorbed in trying to fathom the wiles of Ramadhin saw in Valentine some relief from their discomfort. Valentine, however, in order to keep things tight at his end too, quickened his pace and turned the ball a good deal more with the quickened action, a change in his method of attack which was forced on him by the economy of Ramadhin. Ramadhin would finger the ball with reverence – some said he even talked to it! – on his short walk back, then a quick wheel, a few paces, and down would go another teaser for the batsmen. Alfred Valentine was nearly as quick. Over followed over. Throughout the summer they took 258 first-class wickets, Ramadhin averaging 14.88 runs per wicket and Valentine 17.94. In the Test matches they took 59 wickets, Valentine averaging 20.42 and Ramadhin 23.23.

In the first Test at Old Trafford Valentine took 8 for 104 in the first innings, a record for a bowler making his debut in Test cricket. He

Alfred Valentine, the perfect foil for his partner, and always difficult to score from.

bowled 552 balls (92 overs) in England's second innings at Nottingham – a world record. His total of 33 wickets in four Tests had been exceeded only by S. F. Barnes (34 in 3) against South Africa in 1912. In the second Test at Lord's, Valentine bowled 75 maidens and Ramadhin 70 – both Test records for six-ball overs.

So what is the history of Alfred Valentine? Well, let Jack Mercer, his coach in his early days, tell you what he thought of him:

I knew from the first time that I saw him bowl that he was a 'winner'; and from that time until he came to England he punctually turned up each afternoon with a small case and two old cricket balls. I told him that he must spin it more, and I should not be satisfied until I saw his fingers bleeding. A few days later he turned up with two very bright red fingers carrying the little bag. I don't know where he got the red ink from! I saw him in a Trial match bowling an eight-ball over to an established Test batsman who played at the lot and connected once to mid-off, and that on a billiard table wicket. It was the best piece of bowling I ever saw in a long experience of the game.

Valentine came from a quaint old Spanish town twenty miles out of Kingston, Jamaica and like Ramadhin, he was only twenty years old when he found himself a member of the 1950 West Indies tour party. A writer in *The Cricketer* wrote:

The youngest member of the party, Alfred L. Valentine, has bowled in only two innings in first-class cricket, with figures of 2 for 190, and one might wonder why he is going to England. This left-arm spinner, with his left thumb cocked like a pistol-hammer at the moment of delivery, showed on the unresponsive jute matting in Trinidad that, in addition to being able to bowl a length, he could really spin the ball and get it to turn more than the average left-hander. At the moment his bowling is somewhat mechanical, but a long tour will do a lot to remedy this. Should the wickets give him any help, Valentine may be expected to have a good summer.

Certainly the West Indies selectors thought so, too, and they are to be highly commended for their judgement and their courage. Apparently those who had experienced the West Indies tour to England in 1939 felt that the lack of a left-arm spinner had been a cardinal weakness in their attack, and they were determined to put that right at all costs: even with someone who had just taken 2 for 190! What sort of people were these two, off the field? Let Jeff Stollmeyer tell you another story:

After a game at Southend we were waiting in our coach signing autographs and the coach quickly became surrounded by young autograph hunters. When we moved off there were some disappointed customers, and 'Val', as his team-mates called him, not wanting to disappoint his admirers, plunged his hand deep in his coat pocket and produced innumerable slips of paper on which his name was signed. These he scattered to the four winds and a terrific scramble ensued. This incident was typical of the serious manner in which our two spin bowlers took their autograph commitments. On consecutive nights of the Test match at Trent Bridge they stood outside the hotel in Nottingham and signed their names for well over an hour.

'Ram' came to like England so much that he and his wife now run a pub in Lancashire and he still keeps his spinning fingers supple! We may never see another bowler quite like him. From a distance he could have looked like a mechanical toy as he wheeled away, over after over, but there was nothing mechanical or toy-like about him to the waiting batsmen. He was the greatest illusionist since Houdini!

THE COMEDIANS
CRICKET'S FUNNY MEN

The game of cricket, probably more than any other game, has produced rich humour. Cricket has had its share of funny men. That doesn't mean that if you want to become a comedian you become a cricketer first. If you want to be a comedian you go on the stage. You have to be a good cricketer first and foremost, and then have humour as an important part of your make-up; it's often invaluable in a dressing-room when things aren't going too well. The funny man lifts the spirits of his colleagues when the team is 74 for 9 or when the opponents are 200 for 1. They have been worth their weight in gold over the years. Depressing situations are sometimes not half as bad if you can see the funny side.

Ray East of Essex is probably the best known of the contemporary funny men. In fact he wrote a book last year entitled *A Funny Turn – Confessions of a Cricketing Clown*. Opponents, umpires, colleagues and captains all provide the material for his stories, and he is always able to see a joke against himself:

There was one Essex match in which we made a little bit of cricketing history by having a substitute captaining the side, much to the dismay of the umpires. Keith Fletcher had been injured and was unable to take his place in the team on the first day, a Saturday, but had more or less recovered by Monday. When we were in the field and needed a substitute it was he who came on, and he immediately started to take control. That was just before the tea interval, during which umpire David Evans came over and said that it was not allowed for the captain to be outside the nominated eleven players, as detailed in the very first paragraph of the Laws of Cricket. So after tea we went back into the field and I took with me a piece of paper. Whenever I was setting the field or making a bowling change, I would take out what was in fact a blank sheet of paper and studiously consult it, pretending that 'Fletch' had put it all down in writing for me before we went out again. Fletch played along with it all and we got a nice little routine going whereby I would try to move him and he would either stay where he was, giving meaningful looks with which I would hurriedly concur, or even move in the opposite direction. David Evans himself has a lovely sense of humour and he was quick to appreciate what was going on but he accepted it all in a perfect spirit. After all, can't umpires and captains, enjoy the game, too?'

Ray East, Essex. His book was called *–A Funny Turn – Confessions of a Cricketing Clown.*

145

Ray East told in his book of the day he was bowling to Derek Randall who seemed more fidgety than ever when he was batting, and was whistling, so Ray whistled as he was bowling. This was nothing new. Lancashire had a spin bowler years ago, Cecil Parkin, who frequently whistled the tunes of the day as he was walking back to his mark.

Looking back down the years of cricket history you can always find the funny men, many of them really great cricketers. Among them was George Gunn who played for Nottinghamshire. George hit an elegant 164 on his fiftieth birthday and on another occasion when he hit a hundred in Australia a band played throughout the day. When George got out he said the music had worried him – not because he couldn't concentrate but because he said that when they played a Gilbert & Sullivan selection he thought the cornet was flat! On another occasion he complained to that great cricket writer, Neville Cardus, that he thought cricket was in need of brighter batting. He then went out to bat at Bradford and took nearly four hours in scoring 48. Afterwards George said he hoped Mr Cardus would enjoy his little joke!

George Gunn lived in the game long enough to achieve a remarkable feat. When Notts were playing Warwickshire in 1931 both George, and his son G.C., scored a century in the same innings. George was in his fifty third year; for his son it was his first hundred in first-class cricket. Great cricketer; great humorist.

Probably Australia's funniest man was Arthur Mailey. Arthur began his career as a labourer; he became a leg-break and googly bowler of tantalising flight and spin, a cartoonist, a writer on cricket of rare wit, a painter in oils and, perhaps, most of all, a marvellous companion. It was once said that he played in Test matches because he happened to be walking that way. When, in later years, he became a writer on cricket, his humorous mind was struck by the solemnity of English Press Boxes and once he leaned forward to some of his nearest colleagues and enquired if they would join him in Hymn Number 403! Denzil Batchelor, another distinguished writer, once suggested that Arthur drifted into cricket because he found you stood about for a great deal of the time doing nothing, and not being blamed for it. Arthur wrote, with his customary modesty, that he was not too much of a flop as a youngster. His home-made kites flew better than those of any other lad; the locomotives he made out of old clocks were much admired by other youngsters; with his boomerang he killed snakes out Botany way. When he was twelve for five and sixpence he painted a plaque as a wedding present. He won a boxing bout and a rifle match in the slums, and he stole tomatoes in a Chinese man's market garden and received a good belting for doing so. When he grew up he knew the pains of unemployment. Perhaps his greatest remark was when he was bowling for New South Wales when Victoria scored 1,107 runs. His figures were something in the region of 4 for 360 but Mailey explained that his analysis scarcely did him justice. 'Four catches were dropped off me', he said – 'all by the same man in the pavilion wearing a black hat.'

Fred Trueman combined his ferocious speed with a brand of down-to-earth Yorkshire humour. If he hit a batsman he would always walk down the pitch and enquire 'Are yer still breathing, then?' There is a story about Fred and the Reverend David Sheppard when they were playing together in the England side. Fred and David had very little in common, yet it was always said that they got on together like a house on fire. After David had missed another catch off him in a Test, Fred pleaded, 'For goodness sake put your hands together, Rev, and pray like the rest of us.'

Middlesex once had one of these great humorists, 'Patsy' Hendren. His life brought joy and laughter to all who knew him, and many who didn't. In the deep-field he would always have a conversation going with the spectators. One day he walked into the Surrey dressing-room when Middlesex were playing Surrey at Lord's and saw a youngster he had never seen before getting changed. 'What do you do?' asked Patsy. The youngster was Alf Gover, and he replied, 'I bowl fast'. 'Well,' said Patsy, 'Don't you bowl short at me as I am an old man and I can't see them too well.' So when Alf found himself bowling to Patsy he saw a good chance of getting his wicket. So he bowled short – and every time he did, Patsy hooked him for four. Jack Hobbs walked over to Alf asking 'What do you think you are doing bowling short to him'. Alf told him of the dressing-room conversation. Jack burst out laughing. 'Patsy', he said, 'is the best hooker in the game and you've had your leg pulled.' It was a valuable lesson for Alf, and a nice little joke for Patsy.

Walter Robins, one of Middlesex's great cap-

Keith Fletcher, Captain of Essex, who shared a little joke with comedian Ray East at the umpire's expense.

tains, had a habit of walking towards a spin bowler as the best method of attack, and if he should occasionally miss the ball he carried on walking knowing that the wicket-keeper would have an easy stumping. This happened one day when Patsy was batting at the other end, and when Walter started to walk back to the pavilion Patsy shouted 'He's mssed it'. Walter turned round and threw himself flat on his face trying to regain his ground, but Harry Elliott, the Derbyshire wicket-keeper, had long since whipped the bails off and was chatting to the slips unaware of the little circus episode which Patsy had engineered. Great amusement all round except, apparently, as far as Walter Robins was concerned.

It is interesting that of the funny men we have mentioned so far, three of them are spin bowlers. Perhaps you need a sense of humour as a spinner. Sometimes they take terrible stick from an on form batsman on a wicket giving the bowler little help. Perhaps you need to whistle a little, or laugh at it, as if it doesn't matter in the least, when it matters to you a very great deal.

Cricket today makes much greater physical demands on players than ever it did: seven day a week cricket with an enormous amount of travelling. If you are not a very good side then you are going to have quite a few bad days in seven, and someone in the dressing-room who can lighten the load a bit by seeing the funny side can help weld a team together, could even change the mental attitude and turn a possible defeat into victory. The funny men of cricket are an institution, and what is more, cricket will always need them, come what may.

FLYING STUMPS
It was nearly 50 years ago that these stumps were flying at The Oval – June 1937 – but we have still seen few better photographs of a bowler taking 5 wickets in an innings. The bowler was Eddie Watts of Surrey, he actually took 7 and these were the 5 Essex batsmen he cleaned bowled.

CRICKET IN VERSE

He played his cricket on the heath
The pitch was full of bumps
A fast ball hit him in the teeth,
The dentist drew the stumps.

His record, take it all in all,
Was not a very great one;
He seldom hit a crooked ball
And never stopped a straight one.

'You must keep them on the carpet', is the counsel of the pro.
'And don't leave your ground', he adds, and all agree 'tis so.
Yet even from the pedant, what a deep ecstatic sigh
When the batsman jumps to meet one and a sixer climbs the sky!
E. V. Lucas

A cricketer Lord's bound from Yeovil
Turned up by mistake at the Eovil;
So he said 'Never worry',
And batted for Surrey,
Though this met with some disappreovil.
Dorothy Spring

Mitford! mighty once at cricket,
Head erect and heart elate,
Now alas! he needs no wicket
Save John Bunyan's wicket gate.

Footer has fled and hockey is dead,
But this is no time for repining;
For who can be glum? – the wicket is plumb,
The sun's overhead brightly shining.
So bring out them all, bat, wickets and ball,
And sling me a silly half-volley;
I'll hit it to heaven, and score an eleven –
I feel so uncommonly jolly!

When I was small
My Father began,
With the help of a ball,
To make me a man.

When I was tall
And broad I was glad,
With the help of a ball,
To keep him a lad.
Norman Gale

They had no Grand Stand or Marquee,
Down by the Quarry Farm;
There was a wealth of leafy tree
Behind the bowler's arm.
There were no score-cards to be had,
Cushions for folks to hire:
Only we saw the butcher's lad
Bowl out the village squire

Lord's and the Oval truly mean
Zenith of hard-won fame,
But it was just a village green
Mothered and made the game.
G. D. Martineau

Where else, you ask, can England's game be seen
Rooted so deep as on the village green,
Here, in the slum, where doubtful sunlight falls
To gild three stumps, chalked on decaying walls.

The bat that you were kind enough to send,
Seems (for as yet I have not tried it) good;
And if there's anything on earth can mend
My wretched play, it is that piece of wood.

*This was Cardinal Henry Manning's reply to Charles Wordsworth
upon receiving the present of a cricket bat*

Here lies, bowled out by Death's unerring ball,
A Cricketer renowned, by name John Small.
But though his name was Small, yet great his fame,
For nobly did he play the noble game.

His life was like his innings, long and good,
Full ninety summers he had Death withstood.
At length the ninetieth winter came, when fate
Not leaving him one solitary mate
This last of Hambledonians, old John Small,
Gave up his bat and ball, his leather, wax and all.
Pierce Egan

FEATS, FACTS AND FIGURES

Playing for Surrey against Northamptonshire at Northampton in 1957, Mickey Stewart, now Surrey's cricket manager, took seven catches in Northamptonshire's second innings. No fielder in first-class cricket other than a wicket-keeper had previously taken so many catches in one innings. On a rain-affected wicket Stewart fielded very close to Alec Bedser, Lock and Laker. All ten wickets that fell were caught.

The increase in hits for 6 in the early years of this century is due to the change of scoring laws in 1910. Prior to that date it was necessary to hit the ball out of the ground to score 6, but in 1910 the laws were amended to it being necessary only to hit the ball out of the playing area without bouncing.

The 1938 Test series between England and Australia produced five double centuries: Eddie Paynter (Lancashire) 216 not out; Wally Hammond (Gloucestershire) 240; Len Hutton (Yorkshire) 364; Stan McCabe (Australia) 232; Bill Brown (Australia) 206 not out.

Bill Edrich (Middlesex) had the unusual experience in 1947 against South Africa at Trent Bridge of playing two separate innings before lunch on the same day. He was not out at the start of play and had started his second innings in the follow-on before the adjournment for lunch.

'Gubby' Allen (Middlesex) opened the bowling for England against Australia at Old Trafford in 1934, with a thirteen ball over – three wides, and four no-balls were included.

In the same 1934 Test at Old Trafford, the ball went out of shape and a new one replaced it. In the first over with the replacement ball, Bill O'Reilly took three wickets in four balls.

Denis Atkinson and Clairmonte Depeiza batted throughout the whole of the fourth day for West Indies against Australia in Barbados in 1954–55. They took an overnight total of 187 for 6 to 494 for 6. Atkinson scored 219 and Depeiza 122.

Each of the three Indian players to play for England against Australia scored a century on debut in the series. K. S. Ranjitsinhji scored 154 not out at Old Trafford in 1896; his nephew, K. S. Duleepsinhji scored 173 at Lord's in 1930 and the Nawab of Pataudi scored 102 at Sydney in 1932–33.

How's this for a way of getting out? Andy Ducat, batting for England against Australia at Leeds in 1921, had the shoulder of his bat broken when he played a ball from fast bowler, Ted McDonald; the broken piece of bat dislodged the bails and the ball was caught – a rather different interpretation of caught and bowled.

Three brothers, E.M., W.G., and G.F. Grace all played for England at The Oval in 1880.

Do batsmen have favourite grounds? Yes, they do. One example was Wally Hammond. The ground was Sydney, Australia. In Test matches he scored 251 in 1928–29; 112, 101 and 75 not out in 1932–33; and 231 not out in 1936–37. Denis Compton and Trent Bridge were another high scoring combination, Denis scoring a century on each of his first four Test appearances there and with a batting average of 95.50.

You would think that 500 and more in a first innings was sufficient at least not to lose the match, but there are two instances in Tests between Australia and England and one between Australia and South Africa when the team has lost: Australia 586 at Sydney in 1894–95; England 519 at Melbourne in 1928–29; and Australia 520 against South Africa at Melbourne in 1952–53.

When Miran Bux made his Test debut for Pakistan against India at Lahore in 1954–55 he was forty seven years and 275 days old, but still younger than J. Southerton who, making his debut for England against Australia in Melbourne in 1876–77, was forty nine years 119 days.

There have been two instances of a team scoring over 1,000 runs in an innings: 1,107: Victoria v New South Wales in Melbourne in 1926–27; 1,059: Victoria v Tasmania in Melbourne 1922–23. So Victoria have done it twice on the same ground.

Somerset's bowlers had 1,493 runs scored off them in two consecutive innings at Taunton in 1895: Essex scored 692 and Lancashire 801. In the Lancashire match MacLaren scored 424. In the two innings, Tyler, Somerset's main bowler, took 6 wickets for 427. Lancashire won by an innings and 452 runs.

Now to low scoring. Northamptonshire were all out for 12 against Gloucestershire at Gloucester in 1907. Dennett took 8 wickets for 9 runs including the hat-trick.

Middlesex were all out for 86 against Somerset at Lord's in 1899 – and what happened? They won by an innings and 7 runs. Somerset scored 35 and 44.

Lancashire beat Leicestershire at Old Trafford, Manchester in 1956 without losing a wicket and became the first team in first-class cricket to do so. Leicestershire scored 108 and 122; Lancashire 166 for no wicket declared and 66 for no wicket to win by 10 wickets.

Peter Smith of Essex came in to bat against Derbyshire at Chesterfield in 1947 at number eleven; last man in, he scored 163.

John Inchmore, playing for Worcestershire against Gloucestershire at Cheltenham in 1973, hit 30 in five minutes!

Just a hundred years previously, A. N.Hornby, playing for Lancashire against Surrey at The Oval, scored 10 runs off one ball.

Arthur Wellard of Somerset twice hit five sixes off five consecutive balls in his career, and both on Somerset's ground at Wells, against Derbyshire in 1936 and against Kent in 1938. He hit 72 in 1935; 57 in 1936 and 1938 and 51 in 1933. In those days there was no limit to the length of the boundary.

In contrast Trevor Bailey batted just under six hours to reach 50 for England against Australia at Brisbane in 1958–59.

Godfrey Evans, the Kent and England wicket-keeper, batted for an hour and thirty five minutes before he scored a run for England against Australia at Adelaide in 1946–47.

Glenn Turner of Worcestershire hit 141 not out against Glamorgan at Swansea in 1977 and Worcester were all out for 169.

The highest score for the first wicket by English teams is 555: Percy Holmes and Herbert Sutcliffe for Yorkshire against Essex at Leyton 1932. The highest partnership for the last wicket is 235, F. E.Woolley and A. Fielder for Kent against Worcestershire at Stourbridge in 1909.

'Sonny' Ramadhin, West Indies's famous spin bowler, bowled 98 overs in England's second innings at Edgbaston in 1957 – a total of 588 balls, the most bowled in a single innings.

Mike Procter of Gloucestershire did the hat-trick against Essex at Westcliff in 1972 and against Yorkshire at Cheltenham in 1979 and all six victims were out leg-before-wicket.

Bill Copson, bowling for Derbyshire against Warwickshire at Derby in 1937, took 5 wickets with six consecutive balls. It was Copson's first match after a month out of cricket through injury.

Horace Hazell, bowling for Somerset against Gloucestershire at Taunton in 1949, bowled 105 balls without conceding a run.

In the list of the top twelve bowlers taking the most wickets in an English season, 'Tich' Freeman, Kent's leg-break and googly bowler, appears six times. He heads the list with 304 wickets in 1928; is second with 298 in 1933; is fifth in 1931 with 276; is sixth in 1930 with 275; is eighth in 1929 with 267 and eleventh in 1932 with 253.

George Hirst of Yorkshire holds one remarkable record. Against Somerset at Bath in 1906 he scored a century in each innings (111 and 117 not out) and took 6 for 70 and 5 for 45 – two centuries and eleven wickets.

Frank Woolley, who played for Kent from 1906 to 1938, held over a thousand catches in his career: 1,018 to be exact.

SOME TEST CRICKET RECORDS

HIGHEST INNINGS TOTALS

903–7d	England v Australia (Oval)	1938
849	England v West Indies (Kingston)	1929–30
790–3d	West Indies v Pakistan (Kingston)	1957–58
758–8d	Australia v West Indies (Kingston)	1954–55
729–6d	Australia v England (Lord's)	1930
701	Australia v England (Oval)	1934
695	Australia v England (Oval)	1930
687–8d	West Indies v England (Oval)	1976
681–8d	West Indies v England (Port of Spain)	1953–54
674	Australia v India (Adelaide)	1947–48
668	Australia v West Indies (Bridgetown)	1954–55
659–8d	Australia v England (Sydney)	1946–47
658–8d	England v Australia (Nottingham)	1938
657–8d	Pakistan v West Indies (Bridgetown)	1957–58
656–8d	Australia v England (Manchester)	1964
654–5	England v South Africa (Durban)	1938–39
652	Pakistan v India (Faisalabad)	1982–83
652–8d	West Indies v England (Lord's)	1973
650–6d	Australia v West Indies (Bridgetown)	1964–65

The highest innings for the countries not mentioned above are:

644–7d	India v West Indies (Kanpur)	1978–79
622–9d	South Africa v Australia (Durban)	1969–70
551–9d	New Zealand v England (Lord's)	1973
454	Sri Lanka v Pakistan (Faisalabad)	1981–82

LOWEST INNINGS TOTALS

26	New Zealand v England (Auckland)	1954–55
30	South Africa v England (Port Elizabeth)	1895–96
30	South Africa v England (Birmingham)	1924
35	South Africa v England (Cape Town)	1898–99
36	Australia v England (Birmingham)	1902
36	South Africa v Australia (Melbourne)	1931–32
42	Australia v England (Sydney)	1887–88
42	New Zealand v Australia (Wellington)	1945–46
42†	India v England (Lord's)	1974
43	South Africa v England (Cape Town)	1888–89
44	Australia v England (Oval)	1896
45	England v Australia (Sydney)	1886–87
45	South Africa v Australia (Melbourne)	1931–32
47	South Africa v England (Cape Town)	1888–89
47	New Zealand v England (Lord's)	1958

†*Batted one man short*

The lowest innings for the countries not mentioned above are:

76	West Indies v Pakistan (Dacca)	1958–59
62	Pakistan v Australia (Perth)	1981–82
93	Sri Lanka v New Zealand (Wellington)	1982–83

HIGHEST INDIVIDUAL INNINGS

365*	G. S. Sobers, West Indies v Pakistan (Kingston)	1957–58
364	L. Hutton, England v Australia (Oval)	1938
337	Hanif Mohammad, Pakistan v West Indies (Bridgetown)	1957–58
336*	W. R. Hammond, England v New Zealand (Auckland)	1932–33
334	D. G. Bradman, Australia v England (Leeds)	1930
325	A. Sandham, England v West Indies (Kingston)	1929–30
311	R. B. Simpson, Australia v England (Manchester)	1964
310*	J. H. Edrich, England v New Zealand (Leeds)	1965
307	R. M. Cowper, Australia v England (Melbourne)	1965–66
304	D. G. Bradman, Australia v England (Leeds)	1934
302	L. G. Rowe, West Indies v England (Bridgetown)	1973–74

RECORD WICKET PARTNERSHIPS – ALL TEST CRICKET

1st	413	V. Mankad & P. Roy, I v NZ (Madras)	1955–56
2nd	451	W. H. Ponsford & D. G. Bradman, A v E (Oval)	1934
3rd	451	Mudassar Nazar & Javed Miandad, P v I (Hyderabad)	1982–83
4th	411	P. B. H. May & M. C. Cowdrey, E v WI (Birmingham)	1957
5th	405	S. G. Barnes & D. G. Bradman, A v E (Sydney)	1946–47
6th	346	J. H. W. Fingleton & D. G. Bradman, A v E (Melbourne)	1936–37
7th	347	D. S. Atkinson & C. C. Depeiza, WI v A (Bridgetown)	1954–55
8th	246	L. E. G. Ames & G. O. B. Allen, E v NZ (Lord's)	1931
9th	190	Asif Iqbal & Intikhab Alam, P v E (Oval)	1967
10th	151	B. F. Hastings & R. O. Collinge, NZ v P (Auckland)	1972–73

NINE OR TEN WICKETS IN AN INNINGS

10–53	J. C. Laker, England v Australia (Manchester)	1956
9–28	G. A. Lohmann, England v South Africa (Johannesburg)	1895–96
9–37	J. C. Laker, England v Australia (Manchester)	1956
9–69	J. M. Patel, India v Australia (Kanpur)	1959–60
9–86	Sarfraz Nawaz, Pakistan v Australia (Melbourne)	1978–79
9–95	J. M. Noreiga, West Indies v India (Port of Spain)	1970–71
9–102	S. P. Gupte, India v West Indies (Kanpur)	1958–59
9–103	S. F. Barnes, England v South Africa (Johannesburg)	1913–14
9–113	H. J. Tayfield, South Africa v England (Johannesburg)	1956–57
9–121	A. A. Mailey, Australia v England (Melbourne)	1920–21

F. R. Spofforth	Australia v England (Melbourne)	1878–79
W. Bates	England v Australia (Melbourne)	1882–83
J. Briggs	England v Australia (Sydney)	1891–92
G. A. Lohmann	England v South Africa (Port Elizabeth)	1895–96
J. T. Hearne	England v Australia (Leeds)	1899
H. Trumble	Australia v England (Melbourne)	1901–02
H. Trumble	Australia v England (Melbourne)	1903–04
T. J. Matthews (2)*	Australia v South Africa (Manchester)	1912
M. J. C. Allom†	England v New Zealand (Christchurch)	1929–30
T. W. J. Goddard	England v South Africa (Johannesburg)	1938–39
P. J. Loader	England v West Indies (Leeds)	1957
L. F. Kline	Australia v South Africa (Cape Town)	1957–58
W. W. Hall	West Indies v Pakistan (Lahore)	1958–59
G. M. Griffin	South Africa v England (Lord's)	1960
L. R. Gibbs	West Indies v Australia (Adelaide)	1960–61
P. J. Petherick	New Zealand v Pakistan (Lahore)	1976–77

*In each innings. †Four wickets in five balls.

HIGHEST WICKET-KEEPING DISMISSAL AGGREGATES

Total		Tests	Ct	St
355	R. W. Marsh (A)	96	343	12
269	A. P. E. Knott (E)	95	250	19
228	Wasim Bari (P)	81	201	27
219	T. G. Evans (E)	91	173	46
189	D. L. Murray (WI)	62	181	8
187	A. T. W. Grout (A)	51	163	24
179	S. M. H. Kirmani (I)	78	145	34
162	R. W. Taylor (E)	51	155	7
141	J. H. B. Waite (SA)	50	124	17
130	W. A. S. Oldfield (A)	54	78	52
114	J. M. Parks (E)	46	103	11

N.B. Parks's figures include 2 catches as a fielder.

SOME FIRST-CLASS CRICKET RECORDS

COMPLETE TO END OF 1984 SEASON

Highest Innings Totals

1107	Victoria v New South Wales (Melbourne)	1926–27
1059	Victoria v Tasmania (Melbourne)	1922–23
951–7d	Sind v Baluchistan (Karachi)	1973–74
918	New South Wales v South Australia (Sydney)	1900–01
912–8d	Holkar v Mysore (Indore)	1945–46
910–6d	Railways v Dera Ismail Khan (Lahore)	1964–65
903–7d	England v Australia (Oval)	1938
887	Yorkshire v Warwickshire (Birmingham)	1896
849	England v West Indies (Kingston)	1929–30

NB. There are 22 instances of a side making 800 runs or more in an innings, the last occasion being 951–7 declared by Sind as above.

Lowest Innings Totals

12*	Oxford University v MCC and Ground (Oxford)	1877
12	Northamptonshire v Gloucestershire (Gloucester)	1907
13	Auckland v Canterbury (Auckland)	1877–78
13	Nottinghamshire v Yorkshire (Nottingham)	1901
14	Surrey v Essex (Chelmsford)	1983
15	MCC v Surrey (Lord's)	1839
15*	Victoria v MCC (Melbourne)	1903–04
15*	Northamptonshire v Yorkshire (Northampton)	1908
15	Hampshire v Warwickshire (Birmingham)	1922
16	MCC and Ground v Surrey (Lord's)	1872
16	Derbyshire v Nottinghamshire (Nottingham)	1879
16	Surrey v Nottinghamshire (Oval)	1880
16	Warwickshire v Kent (Tonbridge)	1913
16	Trinidad v Barbados (Bridgetown)	1941–42
16	Border v Natal (East London)	1959–60

*Batted one man short.

NB. There are 26 instances of a side making less than 20 in an innings.